7.99

Reverse Time Travel

.

Reverse Time Travel

Barry Chapman

CASSELL

First published 1995
by Cassell
Wellington House
125 Strand
London
WC2R 0BB

Distributed in the United States
by Sterling Publishing Co., Inc.
387 Park Avenue South, New York, New York 10016-8810

Distributed in Australia
by Capricorn Link (Australia) Pty Ltd
2/13 Carrington Road
Castle Hill
NSW 2154

British Library Cataloguing-in-Publication Data
A catalogue record for this book is available from the British Library
ISBN 0-304-34524-5

Design, Illustrations and Typesetting by Ben Cracknell
Printed and bound in Great Britain by
Butler & Tanner Ltd, Frome and London

Contents

Introduction   7

I   You Are Here   10

II   The Paradox: Science's Springboard   22

III   Newton v. Einstein: A Matter of Relative Importance   33

IV   Distance v. Time: The Fourth Dimension   53

V   FTL   62

VI   General Relativity: A Matter of Some Gravity   69

VII   Black and White Singularities: The Hole Story   79

VIII   Cosmology: In the Beginning   101

IX   Entropy and the Arrow of Time   106

X   Bottomless Seas, Limitless Wells   119

XI   All Physics Is Geometry   129

XII   The Fifth Dimension and the Multiverse   137

Appendix A: Four-Space   148

Appendix B: Entropy   150

Appendix C: Dirac's Derivation of Negative Mass-Energy   151

Appendix D: Complex Relativistic Rotation   152

Bibliography   153

Index   156

*To my daughter, Alexandria,
that she may grow to learn of
wonders the existence of which
we do not even suspect.*

Introduction

The fourth dimension is as real and true a dimension as any of the other three. In fact, they couldn't exist without it. Why is it that we usually ignore the fourth dimension? Because we have no freedom of movement within it. You see, we can move in the other three, up, down, sideways, forwards, backwards... But, when it comes to time, we are prisoners.

MGM film version of H.G. Wells' 1895 novel
The Time Machine

Are we really prisoners of time? The answer in H.G. Wells' time was an unequivocal yes! Each second proceeded irrevocably onwards at a constant pace for everyone. Wells speculated on the possibility of breaking this accepted rule. In his novel, he has his main character build a machine that alters the rate at which its occupant experiences the passage of time, allowing him to travel repeatedly into the far future and back while only minutes elapse for the passenger.

But this vision of time travel has serious faults. Wells' voyager is able to observe the rapid passage of time as he travels into the future, yet the rest of humanity is unable to observe him moving incredibly slowly. In addition, the time machine remains fixed at the same point on the Earth's surface, though why this should be is not made clear. One unfortunate consequence is that, on its return through time, the machine occupies the same space at the same time as it does on the outward journey; in fact, at all points in time. Yet, somehow, it does this without colliding with itself. This is also true of its subsequent journeyings back and forth in time – a remarkable achievement indeed, considering that all the copies of itself are simultaneously careering back and forth in time.

We should not be too critical of the author, however. Wells' work was essentially a social comment, written by an author with a strong historical perspective. The relative passage of time sequences are a natural result of the novel idea of time travel. In all it was a unique vision, and one that is all the more remarkable for having predated the work of Albert Einstein by two decades.

Perhaps this is not so remarkable, for an idea will frequently circulate long before respectable scientists, for fear of being ridiculed, can give credence to it. First, the idea must accumulate a large enough body of supporting evidence to outweigh the accepted view. The classic example is the Roman Catholic Church's opposition to Galileo's fifteenth-century theory of a central sun. Indeed, it was only in the 1990s that the church finally conceded that the Earth did orbit the sun, and not the other way around – a 'fact' that resulted from Aristotle's unquestionable theory of cosmology.

With the publication of Einstein's special theory of relativity in 1905 the prison of time became an open one. Where previously we were trapped inside the rigid framework of Newton's absolute time, special relativity allows us to venture outside our cell – but only a little way. Now we are permitted to move forward in time at a different rate from our fellows, much in the manner of Wells' time traveller. Now, though, we are able to observe him moving at a different rate through time, just as he can us. Yet we remain prisoners, for we must still move only forward and cannot turn the clock back. Einstein's theory also shows that we cannot exceed the speed of light. So, besides being prisoners of time, we are now also confined in space; but more of this later.

Newton's theories of an absolute inflexible time had held sway for several hundred years, just as Aristotle's ideas had dictated the limits of our knowledge for two thousand years before him. These and indeed all our theories form a sort of container into which we carefully fit our observations. Inevitably, the accumulated knowledge becomes too great for the container to hold. New facts simply do not fit the old theories. Patching up the theories serves to hold back the tide of new information for a while, but eventually a new container must be found.

In this book I have catalogued some of the items of current knowledge that do not quite fit within the generally accepted boundaries – part of the growing body of evidence for the possibility of travel backwards in time. I am not alone in questioning the conventional premise that time travel is impossible: several respected cosmologists are also beginning at least to entertain the possibility. In September 1992 the BBC broadcast a radio programme which explored this idea, 'Across the Edge of Time', the first in a new Radio 4 series entitled *High resolution*. I believe that the time is ripe for the certainty of the impossibility of time travel to give way before the growing body of evidence in support of it.

Many of the speculative ideas in this book have been proposed before, some of them several times, as new people have followed the clues which nature provides in abundance. What I have attempted here is to gather together many different strands concerning the central hypothesis of reverse time travel. If only one reader derives a better understanding of nature through exposure to these ideas, the effort will have been worth while.

It might be useful at this point, before we get into the interesting material, to say a word about equations. The text is intended to be self-explanatory and mathematical equations have been kept to a minimum, but, like the diagrams, they form a useful adjunct – an alternative language in which to express ideas. For the most part you can ignore them completely and the text will still make perfect sense. Alternatively, if mathematics is your forte, some of the more central results can be found in the appendices. For those readers who are interested in mathematics, there are a number of excellent books on almost every aspect covered in this one and any library should be able to provide you with a selection. For this reason, with a few exceptions, specific references are not given.

Finally, I would like to say a word concerning the genesis of this work. In 1963, there was a young boy who knew enough special relativity to understand that travel faster than the speed of light is impossible. He was also aware of the vast distances between his small planetary island and even the nearest of its neighbours. This made him very unhappy. In that year a remarkable television series called *Dr Who* was launched in the UK. The central idea was that travel in both space and time (in space-time) was possible. This was a revelation. It gave the young boy hope, a dream to pursue. That young boy exists now only in the past. But the dream lives on.

If we are prisoners of time, it is not because there is a fundamental law preventing us from breaking its bonds. Rather it is simply that we do not yet possess the necessary technology to escape, just as a hundred years ago we could not escape the confines of the Earth. I fervently believe that the scientific evidence demonstrates the possibility of travel in both directions of time. Read on! And make up your own mind.

· I ·
You Are Here

The Total Perspective Vortex is the worst thing that can happen to anybody... For when you are put in the Vortex you are given just one momentary glimpse of the size of the entire unimaginable infinity of creation, along with a tiny little marker saying YOU ARE HERE.

Douglas Adams,
The Hitch Hiker's Guide to the Galaxy

This book is a challenge to the way in which we perceive the world about us, to those boundaries that we ourselves have drawn between the possible of today and the possible of tomorrow. In particular, it questions the certainty with which we proclaim that time, which in all other ways is identical to space, differs in one very important aspect. While for every forward movement there is a backward one, for every left a corresponding right and for every up a down, for time we are only permitted an upwhen, with no corresponding downwhen. We may travel only futurewards, with no possibility of travel pastwards.

I have always felt uncomfortable about this certainty; and about several other anomalies that authorized science is happy to sweep under the carpet. No one enjoys bad publicity, and scientists are no exception. Consequently we tend to ignore, for the time being, those rare failures of our current theories and to concentrate on the numerous successes. However, as will be seen in this chapter, it is often by examining these embarrassing blemishes that we come to a better understanding of the way in which our universe works. And perhaps, during this examination, we may even push back the frontiers of our present understanding a little.

In essence, the frontiers of modern science are the very large and the very small: on one side the boundaries of the universe in both space and time, and on the other the most minute building blocks from which everything in it is constructed. In this sense the frontiers have never really changed, and possibly they never will. Science has pushed back these frontiers and will continue to do so, with an occasional pause for review and reconciliation. This process is one that, by its very nature, may have no end.

Many scientists might not agree with this last statement, for even as our optical telescopes plumb ever further the depths of space, our far infra-red ones are looking back to the beginning of time. At the same time, scientists seem poised finally to uncover the unified field theory that will unite all the laws of physics into a coherent whole; this is a theory for which scientists and mathematicians have been searching for fifty years and more. Many nineteenth-century scientists had somewhat similar ideas about the state of their knowledge; they too believed that they were near to a complete understanding of the physical universe. So before we begin to review our present complacency, it might be useful to examine the bases they had for theirs.

At the end of the last century the universe was perceived to be a cosmic billiards game. Atoms, the smallest building blocks of which everything was believed to be composed, were the perfectly elastic and predictable balls with which the game was being played. In the words of the nineteenth-century scientist Albert Michelson (of whom more later), the only task remaining for twentieth-century scientists was to refine the measurements of the past by adding a few decimal places. Well, we added those few decimal places. On the large scale we obtained Einstein's relativity and with it the virtually limitless power of nuclear energy; and on the small scale we discovered quantum mechanics, which led us to develop transistors, microchips and computers. We also acquired television, superconductivity, travel to the moon and who can say what next. Some of the scientific consequences of these major ideas will be discussed in later chapters.

But all this has rather taken us away from the point of this chapter, which is to give a starting point for our exploration of the boundaries of modern science. Before we can hope to go exploring it is helpful to have some idea of where we are, and also when we are. By this I mean that any starting point should be defined both spatially and temporarily. Where exactly are you at this moment? And what precisely does this moment mean? You are sitting comfortably, or so I would hope, somewhere upon the surface of the planet Earth, somewhen about the end of the twentieth century – at least, in relation to the somewhat arbitrary dating system currently employed in the West. But what exactly do these reference points mean in terms of the universe as a whole? To answer this I shall embark on a brief history of life, the universe and, in fact, everything.

A brief history of everything

The story begins some 15,000 million years ago. Before this? Well, there was no 'before this'. Time, space and everything within it simply came into being at a particular point in space and at a particular moment (the first) in time – at least according to the best theories of the origins of the universe we have to date. For now you will have to take these facts on trust, though we shall be examining the evidence for them a little later. So, at the beginning of space and time everything was contained in a single, infinitely dense core. Immediately afterwards it underwent a rapid expansion, in fact an explosive one. This has given us a rather catchy and fairly accurate name for this theory of the universe's origin – the Big Bang.

Following the Big Bang the vast energy that had been concentrated at a single point rushed off in all directions. I use the term 'energy' deliberately here, for matter could not exist at the unimaginably high temperatures prevalent during this time. In fact, mass and energy are really two manifestations of the same phenomenon, which is precisely the meaning of Einstein's much quoted $E = mc^2$, the potency of which was so dramatically demonstrated at Hiroshima. As the universe expanded further, it cooled, allowing the vast majority of this energy to condense into matter in the form of individual electrons, protons, neutrons and a few trace elements of the more esoteric particles that are occasionally found. By this time the universe was about one ten-millionth of a second old. The expansion continued and with it the cooling. After a few minutes it became cool enough for the individual particles to start associating with each other in some permanent manner, and matter composed of atoms, such as those from which everything about us is composed, came into being. This process of atom building carried on for the next half million years, during which time matter became more important than energy in determining the evolution of the universe.

As this expansion continued still further, local variations in the density of matter caused it to condense, under the action of gravity, into great isolated, rotating dust and gas clouds called proto-galaxies and galactic clusters. The process of condensation continued within these proto-galaxies, and stellar clouds formed. In turn, within the centres of these stellar clouds stars condensed. Further out in these stellar clouds,

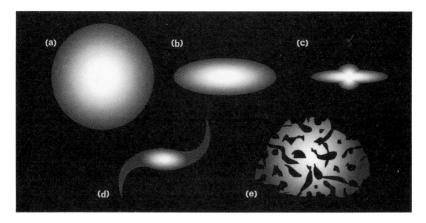

Fig. 1.1 Types of galaxy. (a) spherical, (b) elliptical, (c) disc, (d) spiral and (e) irregular

where the mass was insufficient to initiate the fusion processes that power stars, planets formed. And so there came into being proper galaxies, vast collections of isolated stellar systems, in a variety of shapes including spherical, elliptical, disc, spiral and irregular (see Fig. 1.1).

These things are still around today; indeed we live in one, the Milky Way. The reason for its name is immediately apparent to anyone fortunate enough to be able to view the night sky in the absence of clouds, street lights and air pollution.

The life and times of a typical galaxy

Like everything else, galaxies evolve with time. Typically, they begin with a roughly uniform spherical distribution of stellar systems. Usually, in addition to the random motions of the individual stars that comprise a galaxy (see Fig. 1.2), there is a rotation of the whole system about its common centre of mass. If this were not so, all the stars would collapse into this centre in a relatively short time. Fortunately, it requires only a slight motion in any other direction for a star to take up a stable orbit about this common centre.

In time, the stars outside the plane of rotation are drawn into it, and the forces of friction retard their motion back out. Similarly, friction also causes matter to concentrate towards the centre of the galaxy (see Fig. 1.3). The end product is a rotating disc with a bulge in the centre (see Fig. 1.4). The stars that are nearer the centre of this disc orbit faster than those further out. This often results in the creation of the spiral form that is typical of many galaxies, our own included (see Fig. 1.5).

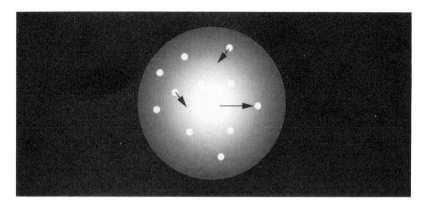

Fig. 1.2 Random stellar motions.

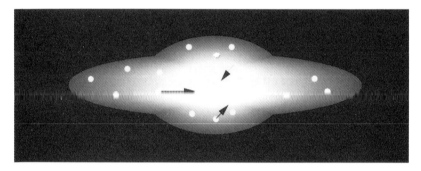

Fig. 1.3 Stellar matter becoming entrapped in what is known as the galactic accretion disc in the centre of the galaxy.

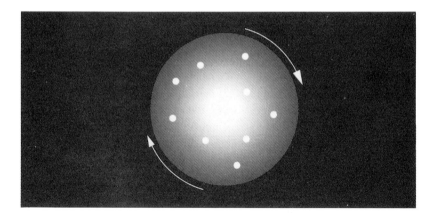

Fig. 1.4 Rotating disc.

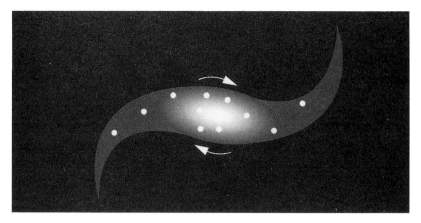

Fig. 1.5 Rotating spiral galaxy.

So it was that the universe evolved, giving rise to the galaxies that still exist today. By the time these galaxies had formed, some 2000 million years had passed since the beginning. Within the galaxies themselves the process of gravitational condensation continued, giving rise to stellar systems containing stars and planets with the greatest concentration of mass occurring at the centre. Now with all that matter rushing together under the action of gravity the temperature rises to create local reversal of the global cooling due to expansion. Eventually this matter reaches a sufficiently high temperature to begin shining, and forms a star at the heart of the stellar system.

The life and times of a typical star

Stars too are mortal. They are born, grow old and die. In their youth the collapse of matter towards the centre of the system creates sufficient heat to cause fusion of hydrogen to form helium. As the supply of hydrogen is exhausted small stars slowly fade away, cooling to form dense, feeble stellar cinders. Larger stars switch over to the fusion of helium into carbon; and when the helium is exhausted, the fusion continues up the periodic table to form all the heavier elements. The entire life cycle of a star is determined by its mass alone. Now some of these stars die quietly, while others – the so-called novas and supernovas – go out in a blaze of glory. Later new stars form, incorporating part of the material from the dying ones.

After about 4000 million years the solar system, our stellar system, condensed; the planets formed from the matter that was too far out and had too much rotational velocity to become part of the sun. Just as stars arrange themselves in a common galactic plane of rotation, and for exactly the same reasons, so too did the planets in the solar system.

Initially the planets were also very hot, again due to the vast energy generated by all that matter falling together. Unlike stars, though, planets have insufficient mass to sustain the intense temperatures necessary for nuclear fusion. Consequently the planets cooled down rapidly, at least by interstellar standards, and are visible today only by dint of reflected sunlight. Eventually one of these planets, the third one out from the sun, became capable of sustaining a peculiar process called life.

There is no reason to suppose that our stellar system is in any way special, so it is reasonable to suppose that the story of its formation has been repeated many times – that many stars, if not the majority, have planets orbiting them. Unfortunately, the distances to even our nearest neighbours are so great that we cannot see the tiny, dim planets even with our largest telescopes. Anything big enough to be seen over inter-stellar distances is massive enough to become a star, forming a binary, tertiary or higher order system; many of these are known. However, a few tentative identifications of very massive planets orbiting other stars have been made, by dint of the effect of their orbiting mass on the stars' motions.

In all this time the universe had continued to expand, as it does still. The mass-energy in it, the galaxies and galactic clusters, everything on the large scale continues to rush away from everything else. It is this that provides us with the main evidence for this description of our origins, so it is therefore worth while looking at the evidence in some detail.

The red shift

First, let's establish a few essential facts about light. This information will also prove useful later as, quite apart from its central role in our ability to observe our environment, light plays a fundamental part in the operation of the universe. Now light is just the name we give to a specific type of electromagnetic radiation. Basically, the nature of all electromagnetic radiation – gamma rays, X-rays, ultra-violet, visible light, infra-red, microwaves, radio waves and so on – is the same. They are all a wave motion, and all travel at exactly the same speed in vac-uum: 186,000 miles or 300,000 kilometres per second. The difference between these various types of electromagnetic radiation lies entirely in their frequency – the number of waves that reach you each second;

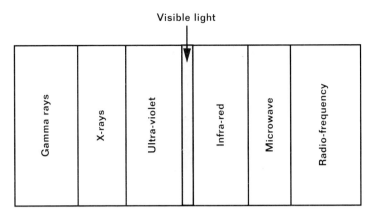

Fig. 1.6 Electromagnetic spectrum (logarithmic scale).

or equivalently, in the length of each of these waves. The greater this frequency, and the shorter the wave, the more energetic the radiation. These differences in the small band of frequencies that we call visible light give us colour (see Fig. 1.6).

One surprising thing is that the speed of light is always the same, independent of the velocity of the source or of the observer; but more of that later. For now it is enough to know that whoever measures it always arrives at the same value. What does change, when either source or observer is moving, is the frequency – the rate at which successive wave crests arrive. Imagine the buffeting of a surfer by the ocean's waves. On his way out he swims through wave after wave, but on the way back he encounters far fewer; only one if he is proficient. The same thing occurs with all wave propagation. This accounts, for example, for the difference in frequency of the sound from a train's whistle depending on whether it is approaching us or going away from us. If we are drawing nearer the source the frequency increases, and if we are drawing away from it the frequency decreases. This is exactly what happens with light: if you and the source are moving towards one another then the rate at which the crests reach you, the frequency, is greater than if the source was at rest relative to you. Similarly, the more rapidly you and the source move apart the lower the frequency.

Let's look now at the experimental evidence of the expansion of the universe. When astronomers first analysed the light from stars in distant galaxies they discovered something very odd: the stars of other galaxies were unlike any of those in our own galaxy. Worse still, the stars in different galaxies were also unlike each other. The analyses themselves were in the form of spectra, plots of the intensity of the electromagnetic radiation at each frequency of which the light is composed. The principle of this analysis is demonstrated beautifully by raindrops which, when illuminated by sunlight, split it into its component spectra. This we see as a rainbow.

The spectrum of a particular star indicates precisely what nuclear reactions are going on inside it to produce the light – that is, what fusion reactions are powering the star, and what other elements are present within it. When astronomers started looking at the spectrum of nearby stars – those in our own galaxy – they found that they fell into several categories according to their size and colour. This is not at all surprising, for a star's size is related to its mass and this determines to a large degree what reactions are going on inside it. So if the spectra of stars in other galaxies are very different from those in our own, then very different processes must be occurring inside them.

Now the light from distant objects has taken a considerable length of time to reach us; it therefore left those stars a long time ago. We know that over long periods of time some stars converted from hydrogen fusion to helium fusion, and on up the periodic table to form the progressively heavier elements. So even if the processes going on in them now are the same as those in our near neighbours, could it not be that, long ago when the light we see now left them, different processes were occurring? The answer is no. Not only did the spectra from stars in other galaxies not fit any conceivable process, but the further away the galaxy the smaller the number of stars within it that exhibited hydrogen fusion. The significance of this lies in the fact that stars must work their way up the hierarchy of fusion reactions. Our own sun, for instance, is still in the earliest hydrogen-to-helium stage. Consequently, as astronomers look further out into the more distant past they should see hydrogen fusion becoming more, not less, frequent.

In 1963 the astronomer Schmidt hit upon the answer. The stellar spectra from distant galaxies are similar to those from stars in our own, but the frequencies are shifted and stretched. In these spectra, visible light is shifted towards the red, lower-frequency, end. It is as if we are looking at a rainbow in which green has taken the place of blue, yellow the place of green, and so on throughout the entire spectrum (see Fig. 1.7). The phenomenon is known as the red shift, and it was for this reason that stellar spectra were not recognized.

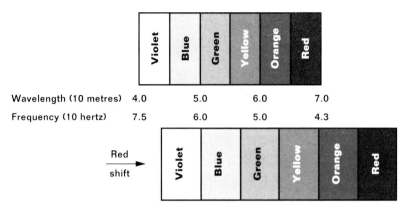

Fig. 1.7 Red shift. When the source is receding, the entire electromagnetic spectrum is stretched and shifted, with the visible part shifting towards the red. All wavelengths become longer and frequencies shorter.

For stellar spectra this shifting and stretching extends beyond the visible spectrum in both directions, throughout the entire range of electromagnetic radiation. Such a shift can be explained quite simply: it occurs whenever either the source or the receiver of the light is moving. The observed red shift corresponds to a lowering of the frequency, and, as we saw earlier, this leads to the conclusion that distant galaxies are moving away from us.

The Hubble constant

Astronomers also discovered that the more distant the galaxy, the greater this red shift; and consequently, the faster the galaxy is retreating from us. In fact, the rate at which the galaxies are moving away is in direct proportion to their distance – one kilometre per second for every 50,000 light years. And this holds true for every direction. This is known as the Hubble constant, after the astronomer who first correctly analysed the data. This constant expansion factor also holds true for any other observer who may inhabit any of these distant galaxies. So the galaxies are rushing away from one another, like the particles in an expanding dust cloud all of which are hurtling apart.

An electromagnetic wave front, originating from the point we now occupy at the beginning of time, would have been moving away at the speed of light ever since. This wave front would represent the furthest extent of the universe. Equivalently, we could say that the universe has been expanding at the speed of light since the beginning of time.

On this basis it is now some 30,000 million light years wide – though this is a flat measure and the meaning of 'wide' depends on the geometry of the universe. We shall be returning to the problem of the universe's geometry in later chapters.

Above, I have referred frequently to a light year. This is simply the distance that light travels in one year. The reason we use this measure of distances is that space is vast. For example, the moon is 400,000 kilometres away, just a mere $1\frac{1}{3}$ light seconds when we remember that light travels at 300,000 kilometres (186,000 miles) per second. In these units the distance to Venus, our nearest neighbour, is $2\frac{1}{2}$ light minutes at its closest; to the sun 8 minutes; to Pluto, the furthest planet in our stellar system, $5\frac{1}{2}$ hours; and to the nearest star over 4 light years or 220 million kilometres. This is why we use the light year as our unit of measurement. Anything else would involve excessively large numbers – like measuring the distance between London and Paris in millimetres! And these are just local distances. Our galaxy for instance is 80,000 light years across and 2 million light years from its nearest neighbour. So it goes on, throughout all space, to the limit of 30 thousand million light years.

Background radiation
There is in addition other, more recent, evidence for the Big Bang. As the mass-energy of the universe became more spread out, it cooled. Since we know roughly how large it has become, we can predict how cold it should be by now. The result is that the universe should be at approximately 3°K (about −270°C). This is the average background temperature; the odd hot spot such as the Earth or even the sun is both rare and exceptional in terms of space as a whole.

During the 1980s and early 1990s equipment of sufficient sensitivity to measure this background radiation was developed, and the result when we look in any direction is indeed 3°K. From these measurements, maps have been made of those first few moments; at present they are fairly crude, but don't forget we are looking back 15,000 million years. This background radiation, then, is the remnant of the Big Bang, an echo of it that has been reverberating throughout the universe since the beginning of time.

Now!
That concludes the main evidence for the Big Bang, and pretty convincing it is. At the present time there is no better theory to explain the

observations. The controversies that remain concern only the details and not the theory itself. For example, from a wide variety of observations and theories the best estimate of the age of the universe lies somewhere between 10 and 20 thousand million years, and I have simply chosen the median value of 15 thousand million years. The actual value may not be known for some time, but the consensus remains that the universe is of a definite, finite age. That the Big Bang did occur, and that its expansion continues and will continue for some time, is not in doubt.

Winding the clock back has given us our best theories of the size, origin and evolution of the universe. So where does that leave us? Well, here we sit, a tiny collection of matter upon the surface of the third planet of a stellar system. At the centre of this system lies a fairly typical star. The whole orbits somewhere in the outer reaches of the Milky Way, itself a vast collection of similar stellar systems. This in turn is just one isolated galaxy amongst a local cluster of galaxies; which in turn is just one cluster amongst many. It is one vast whole, all parts of which are hurtling away from each other at unimaginable speeds. The distances involved are beyond human comprehension. The time is some 15,000 million years, 200 million lifetimes, from the beginning.

YOU ARE HERE

· II ·

The Paradox:
Science's Springboard

*In an infinite universe every possibility, no matter how
unlikely, must be realized somewhere. Therefore there
is a planet somewhere on which you are rich, one even
where you are a king. Alternatively, there must also be
a world where you are a tramp, one where you are a
murderer and one where even now you are dying
a slow agonizing death.*

Essence of a brief item on
BBC TV's *Tomorrow's World*

*It is known that there is an infinite number of worlds but
that not every one is inhabited. Therefore there must be
a finite number of inhabited worlds. Any finite number
divided by infinity is as near to nothing as makes no
odds. So if every planet in the universe has a population
of zero then the entire population of the universe
must also be zero.*

Douglas Adams,
The Hitch Hiker's Guide to the Galaxy

Time travel is impossible. Ask anyone. Request proof and they will
probably give you some variation on the following argument. If time
travel were possible, then a man could travel back in time and murder
his own father before he had fathered his time-travelling son. This pre-
sents the son with a slight problem in that he never existed. But if he
never existed he could not have murdered his father. In which case his

father would have lived to father him. In which case the son would have been able to travel back … and so on.

This self-contradictory sequence is a paradox; and, thankfully, nature abhors paradoxes. They simply do not occur, or at least we have been lucky enough, so far, never to have encountered one. For the time being paradoxes remain within the confines of our boggled imaginations.

This argument illustrates the essence of the major objection to travel backwards in time – the contravention of causality. Clearly, for the writer of a book about time travel it poses a major problem – one that I do not wish to tackle just yet. Not that I believe it to be insurmountable, but the ideas which enable such a powerful argument to be countered will take me some time to develop.

Lying Cretans

The concept of the paradox has been around a long time. The ancient Greeks devised one that became so famous that it is still in use now, some two thousand years later. It goes something like this: Epimenides stated that everything said by any Cretan was a lie. Unfortunately, Epimenides himself was a Cretan. Now if he was telling the truth, then the statement must be a lie. So Epimenides was lying, but then the statement must be true. So Epimenides must be telling the truth, but then … and so on. This, then, is the paradox: if Epimenides is telling the truth he is lying, and if he is lying he is telling the truth! Is that correct? As it turns out, no. A single instance of a Cretan telling the truth invalidates Epimenides' statement. There is in fact no paradox, though for a long time it was believed that there was. Even today, when first presented with this problem few people see through the apparent contradiction immediately.

The general rule is that the opposite of 'every' is 'some', and not 'all'. Hence 'Everything said is a lie' has the logical opposite 'Something said is true', and not 'Everything said is true.' Convinced? If not, suppose that Epimenides made two statements: the first 'I am Epimenides', which is plainly true, and the second 'Everything said by any Cretan is a lie'. The second statement is obviously a lie, since at least one statement made by a Cretan – Epimenides' first one above – was true. Hence there is no paradox! This type of analysis forms part of any course in logic. What was once a bane of ancient Greece's intellectual elite is now no more than a standard textbook example, albeit in an important branch of human knowledge.

The problem posed by Epimenides can be made a little more complicated by blending his two statements into one, to form the new paradox: 'This statement is a lie.' For this there is no such simple logical solution; yet it too has been shown not to be a paradox – though the resolution of this problem involves the nature of statements about statements, rather than statements about reality. Essentially, this new statement generates an infinite series of statements about statements, each of which is alternately true and false. A complete analysis of this latter 'paradox' can be found in books on general semantics, in particular *Science and Sanity* by the twentieth-century philosopher Korzybsky.

These examples are somewhat exotic. While they are quite valuable in their way, they deal in abstractions rather than reality, words rather than physical quantities. Fortunately, the history of physical science is liberally smattered with paradoxes. One of the most famous, and one that also happens to be relevant to later sections of this book, is that of Olbers.

Olbers' paradox

In the early 1800s the astronomer Olbers became disturbed by the darkness of the night sky. It seemed that, not only should the night sky be as bright as the daytime one, but both should be considerably brighter than they are. In fact, in a uniform infinite universe – which is what most scientists of that time believed ours to be – the sky should be infinitely bright.

To follow Olbers' reasoning we have to understand the axioms upon which this apparent paradox is based. Axioms are assumptions that, in the absence of complete information about a system, we must adopt in order to make any headway in describing it. Theories are then developed from the axioms, and these are used to design experiments to test the invalidity of the axioms. It is perhaps ironic that it is the invalidity and not the validity of the axioms that can be tested. This is a fundamental principle of the scientific method, and Epimenides' (so-called) paradox is a prime example. Where it required only one case of a lie to demonstrate the fallacy of Epimenides' statement, it would require the examination of every statement made by every Cretan to demonstrate its truth. For the scientist this means that, where one counter-observation is all that is needed to invalidate a set of axioms, their proof would require a complete experimental verification of all possibilities. For statements about the physical universe, this is clearly a monumental undertaking.

There is a second, highly relevant reason for examining the axioms involved in the understanding of Olbers' paradox. Some of these axioms are common to many models of the universe that are under active investigation today, and which we will encounter later in this book.

Let's take these axioms one at a time. First, and perhaps most important, was the axiom that the laws of physics are the same throughout all space and time. This axiom is still commonly employed. Indeed, it is difficult to imagine holding any other view, for if we did we would have no way of determining anything outside our immediate spatial and temporal observation sphere. If we accept this assumption we can feel confident that any physical law that we discover locally, such as the nature of gravity and of light and the laws of motion, will hold globally throughout the entire universe and throughout all time. It may seem that there are two assumptions being made here, one about space and one about time, but for our present purposes no such distinction need be made. Indeed, as will be seen in later chapters, the natures of space and time are such that no distinction need ever be made.

The second of Olbers' axioms is that the universe is Euclidean, or flat. This means that it goes on indefinitely in all three directions, forwards-backwards, left-right and up-down. Like the first axiom this too may seem indispensable, but it turns out not to be so. How then can space have shape? An analogy will help to answer this question. Consider the surface of the world on which we live. Our not too distant ancestors believed the Earth to be essentially flat apart from the odd mountain lump and oceanic depression. This is a natural enough assumption without the aid of satellite pictures or other, more subtle, observations. Even today we draw flat, Euclidean maps over which we print a square Cartesian lattice for the purpose of small-scale local navigation. Yet if we attempt to map the entire land surface on a flat sheet we are forced to distort the continental outlines, and distances in general, to account for the curvature in three dimensions. In precisely the same way the universe might be, and as we shall see in later chapters probably is, curved in some higher dimension. At the time of Olbers, the idea that the universe was anything other than flat was, quite literally, unthinkable.

Olbers' third axiom was that we live in a typical part of the universe. There is no reason to suppose that we live in some special part of the universe – for example the centre of all the matter that exists. Yet the stars appear very evenly distributed throughout the sky when viewed through even the most powerful telescopes. It followed, according to Olbers, that the density of matter throughout all space is a constant, and is the same as that which we measure locally – in other words, that the amount of matter in suitably large volumes is the same everywhere. The need for large volumes is obvious when one considers the variation in the density of matter in the immediate vicinity of, for example, a typical room. The density of this book, for instance, is very much greater than the air between it and the reader. Note that this axiom is not the same as the first. The laws could be the same everywhere and we could still inhabit an unusual region – for example, one in which there was a greater local concentration of stars than anywhere else.

Finally, the scientists of Olbers' time assumed that the universe was basically static – that the large-scale density did not change with time. This may at first seem a little strange, since Newton's law of gravitation, of which they were very much aware, might suggest that the attraction of the stars would eventually pull everything together. Olbers and his contemporaries argued that the presence of unending uniformly dense matter in all directions provides for an equal pull in every direction. Consequently, they said, the forces on a global scale balanced out, allowing the local additional attractions to dominate. But there is an overwhelming problem with this argument – this uniform gravitational background is infinite. Amazingly, such an objectionable state of affairs was glossed over, though eventually it was to become one of the major stumbling blocks of all such infinite Euclidean models of the universe.

We are now in a position to derive Olbers' result that night and day should be equally bright. Now the intensity of the light we receive from a star diminishes with the distance we are from it. The reason for this is that the light from a star expands on a spherical wave front, similar to the expansion of a balloon as it is inflated. As this sphere expands, the energy of the wave is spread out over an increasingly large surface area. Therefore the amount falling on a particular area, such as the eye of any observer, is less as the wave spreads out. This gives us a precise relationship for the diminishing of light with distance from the source. It is simply the inverse of the surface area of a sphere,

$$\frac{I}{(4\pi \, r^2)}$$

where r is the distance to the source and I is the intensity at a distance from an average star where the corresponding area is one.

Now the number of stars in a thin shell at a distance r from us is given by the product of the average star density ρ with the volume of the shell, i.e.

$$4\pi r^2 \rho \, \Delta r$$

where Δr is the shell thickness (see Fig. 2.1). The number of stars at a given distance, then, is proportional to the surface area of a sphere at this distance.

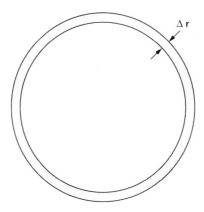

Fig. 2.1 Olbers' stellar shells.

The total amount of light we receive from all the stars in a shell is just the amount we get from one star, multiplied by the total number of stars in that shell:

$$I \, \rho \, \Delta r$$

which is a constant. (In other words, the light we receive is the same for every shell). The total amount of light falling on the Earth is just the sum of the light from every shell. But, in an infinite universe, there are an infinite number of shells, so the total intensity must also be infinite. As these shells surround us completely, both day and night should be infinitely bright.

Plainly this is not true. So where did we, or rather Olbers, go wrong? The more mathematically inclined reader may have spotted that the equation $4\pi r^2 \, \rho \, \Delta r$ is only approximate, but if we perform this calculation using exact calculus methods the result is exactly the same. There is in fact nothing whatsoever wrong with the reasoning. This is Olbers' paradox.

The same reasoning can be applied to gravity, for gravity obeys the same inverse square law as light; the only difference is in the intensity in the constant in the above equations. Following the above arguments again results in the conclusion that there should be an infinite gravitational background. In Olbers' time the infinities for the subtle force of gravity could be politely ignored, or, as we saw, reasoned away. The same argument could not be used for something as glaringly obvious as light. There is no way that an infinite amount of light could be falling upon our delicate retinas, while simultaneously we were observing small finite local variations.

Other attempts were made to explain away Olbers' paradox within the framework of the accepted axioms. For instance, the space between the stars is filled with interstellar dust. This, it was argued, would absorb some of the light from distant stars, much as clouds here on Earth diminish the sun's light. Unfortunately, after a very short time this interstellar dust would become very hot from all the light energy it had absorbed. It would then begin re-emitting light at an ever-increasing rate until it was emitting energy as fast as it was receiving it. So we are rapidly back to our starting point. Though many more attempts of increasing ingenuity were made to patch up the existing theories, none proved successful.

To resolve Olbers' paradox, we are forced to question the assumptions upon which the results are based. This step proved very difficult for both the scientists of Olbers' day and those succeeding them for some considerable time afterwards. Let's now take a fresh look at these axioms with a view to discovering which of them can be dispensed with. The first axiom, that the laws of physics are the same everywhere, we shall retain. Otherwise we can make no headway.

The second axiom, that the universe is flat, may indeed not be true. If, like the surface of the Earth, it forms a closed curve in some higher dimension, then its total size becomes finite and the total stellar energy may well be finite. Unfortunately, the rate of energy dispersion in such a universe is less than that given by the inverse square law for Euclidean spaces. In addition, if this light misses us the first time around, it will continue circling the universe until it gets back to us. Once again we find ourselves in a paradoxical situation. Alternatively, the universe could be curved in the opposite sense. This is a little more difficult to imagine, but none the less possible. In this case, the intensity of light both never returns and diminishes more rapidly than in a flat universe. This, then, would resolve the paradox. Unfortunately, the only long-range curving effect we know of is gravity, and, as we will see later, this acts to curve space back on itself in precisely the wrong way for our purposes. In order for space to curve the other way, we would have to assume some repulsive force which, although exceedingly weak, diminishes less rapidly than the inverse square relationship which governs gravity. Such a force would, at sufficient distance, over-ride the effect of gravity and 'bend' space in the necessary way. Unfortunately there is no experimental, observational or theoretical evidence to support the existence of such a force of repulsion, and so we shall reject this also.

The third axiom, that we live in a typical part of the universe, is, as we have seen previously, borne out by our observation. We have no very good reason for dropping this one.

Let us turn then to the final axiom, that the universe is static. As already observed, there are problems associated with this idea, in that it results not only in an infinite amount of light, but also in an infinite gravitational background. It is this axiom, then, that we must reject. But in rejecting a static universe we must now ask: how does the universe change with time? Since all matter exerts an attractive force on all other matter, we might expect the universe to be collapsing. Certainly we would expect a universe that was initially at rest to collapse. Unfortunately, in such a universe Olbers' paradox arises with even greater ease.

We are left with the possibility of a universe in which all the matter is spreading out in every direction, getting thinner – less dense – with time. In such a universe, the energy reaching us from successive stellar shells is progressively weaker. Consequently, the total energy we receive remains not only finite, but quite small enough to allow for the observed difference between night and day. So Olbers can rest in peace, in the sure knowledge that he, and indeed the whole Earth, will not be suddenly vaporized by an infinite amount of energy blazing forth from the night sky.

Once more we have succeeded in resolving what was an apparently paradoxical situation. In an expanding universe Olbers' paradox simply does not occur. The night sky is dark because the light coming from the more distant stars has been weakened by their recession. The red shift, which we encountered in Chapter 1, represents precisely this loss in energy from distant objects. Concluding that this was due to the retreat of distant objects may seem obvious in the light of our solution to Olbers' paradox, but the discovery of the red shift during the last half-century actually preceded the resolution of the paradox. Such is our reluctance to give up old ideas. Olbers' paradox also provides us with a valuable insight into the way in which objections to scientific theories are dealt with. It is particularly interesting given the fact that at least one modern theory – to be encountered in Chapter 11 – also requires us to accept an infinite global gravitational background.

Before we go on to consider other paradoxes let's look again at Olbers' other axioms in the light of the resolution of his paradox, for it is worth while ensuring that we have not generated any new ones. As far as the first axiom is concerned, an expanding universe certainly poses no problems for the consistency of the laws of physics. The second axiom, that the universe is flat, has already been discarded; as yet, no one is in a position to make any final statement on the shape of the universe, though we shall be making a good attempt later. Now the third axiom, that we live in a typical part of the universe, needs some careful thought. For, as all distant matter is hurtling away from the Earth, it follows from this axiom that the same is true for any hypothetical observer and every distant receding object (see Fig. 2.2).

If we extend this idea in a straight line out from the Earth in any direction we come to the conclusion that the more distant an object, the faster it is receding from us. But in an infinite, flat, Euclidean universe the most distant objects would have to be moving away at infinite speeds, and this creates a whole series of new problems. It is hardly surprising that scientists and philosophers were unwilling to accept this solution to the problem before the discovery of experimental evidence in the form of the red shift. Fortunately, in curved universes there is no such problem. The simplest demonstration is provided by our earlier analogy of the surface of a sphere, except that the surface of the Earth is now replaced by a partially inflated balloon. If we use a series of dots on this balloon to represent galaxies, then, as

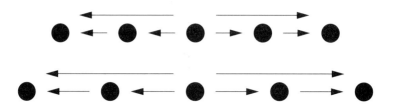

Fig. 2.2 Receding objects.

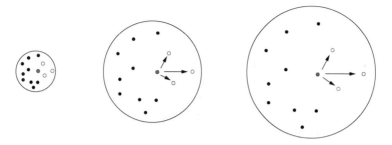

Fig. 2.3 Recession on the surface of an expanding balloon.

we blow the balloon up, each of these galaxies moves away from the others, and the further away they are the faster they separate (see Fig. 2.3). All observers perceive similar recessions, while at all times the model remains finite. For the real universe we would need a four-dimensional, hyperspherical balloon, but the analogy holds. This is in fact an extremely useful analogy, to which we shall return often in later chapters.

One other important point should be noted from this analysis of Olbers' paradox: beware of infinities! Infinity is an extremely useful mathematical concept. It is also a very valuable tool for the construction of paradoxes. This should be immediately apparent from the two examples with which this chapter opened. There are many spoof mathematical 'proofs' involving infinity, and readers would be advised to be very wary of any argument which involves either it, or its inverse zero.

Time travel

Let's have another look at the statement with which this chapter opened: 'Time travel is impossible.' Implicit in the arguments against this statement is that it is travel backwards in time that is meant. Plainly time travel forwards in time is possible. If you do not believe this, try to stop moving forwards in time for a minute. Did you succeed? If so, how did you time yourself? This is not a joke but quite a serious problem when talking about time, and one that has given rise to much confusion over the eighty or so years since Einstein first enlightened us to its relative nature. Previously, time and space had been the great absolutes. In other words, no matter who measured them they obtained the same values provided that his or her clock and ruler were working correctly. Einstein showed that this was not always the case. When two such observers are moving relative to one another, both their rulers and clocks will disagree. Halt them relative to one another, and subsequently their rulers will agree and their clocks will run at the same rate. Einstein went much further than just making this rather negative assertion, producing a theory that accounts for this result and enables any two observers to 'correct' for the discrepancies.

At first Einstein's ideas, particularly those concerning relative time, were strongly resisted. The concept of a flexible time ran counter to everyday experience, but this is only because the effect is so small at the speeds normally encountered that only the most accurate of present-day measuring apparatus can even begin to detect it. Before long several 'paradoxes' arising from these theories were discovered. Naturally they were all resolved; Chapter 3 illustrates one or two of them. But Einstein did not stop there; he went on to develop general relativity, which introduces a sense of gravity into the proceedings. For gravity too affects both the local passage of time, and distance. Quite simply, general relativity states that the space and time distortion due to gravity is exactly equivalent to that experienced during acceleration; more of this later.

All these examples show that what formerly appeared to be paradoxes have subsequently been resolved; and that the occurrence of a paradox has frequently revealed some fallacy in our understanding of the way in which the universe works. Finally, and perhaps most importantly, the resolution of these paradoxes has almost invariably resulted in a better understanding of the nature of the physical universe.

Paradoxes are a kind of gauntlet that our own theories cast at our feet. They challenge us to resolve them and thereby gain a deeper insight into the mysteries which surround us. We decline these challenges at the peril of our continued ignorance.

If, for the moment, we are willing to suspend our disbelief in time travel, then perhaps the paradox with which this chapter opened can also be resolved. To what new insights into reality might this lead us?

· III ·

Newton v. Einstein: A Matter of Relative Importance

Run in a straight line for 10 seconds at 10 metres per second and you will find yourself 100 metres from the point at which you started. The distance is just the velocity multiplied by the time, $s = v\,t$. Both you and anyone else who was watching you would agree on all three quantities, whether they were running along with you, standing still or moving in any fashion. This is Newtonian relativity, and it really is that simple. It is expressed mathematically by the following set of transformation equations:

$$x' = x$$
$$y' = y$$
$$z' = z - v\,t$$
$$t' = t$$

where x, y, z, t are the space and time coordinates measured by a stationary observer, and x', y', z', t' are those measured by an observer moving at velocity v in the positive z direction relative to him (see Fig. 3.1).

Einstein's special relativity states that these equations are not quite correct – that for different inertial observers (observers who are in uniform relative motion) measurements of both distance and time will differ. It also provides a means of calculating the correct values for every observer. Unfortunately, the calculations for the more accurate results of special relativity are also more complicated than Newton's. For this reason we continue to use Newton's relativity when the errors are extremely small, which is true in most everyday situations. For instance, in the above example the error is far too small to show up on the ten- or twelve-digit display of the average calculator. Additionally, the error in any real measurement, the tiny variations in speed and so on, will far outweigh the minute differences in the results of the two calculations.

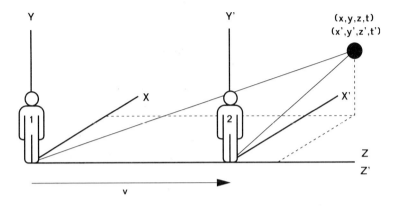

Fig. 3.1 The coordinates of the same point measured by two observers in motion relative to each other.

So why is Einstein's special relativity used, and how do we know it is the correct one of the two? Well, at high speeds, over long distances and over long periods of time, the errors in Newtonian relativity accumulate to the point where they are apparent. In addition, Newtonian relativity completely fails to account for the constancy of the speed of light.

The constancy of the speed of light

In the face of the relative nature of motion, how is it that light can have an absolute velocity? Perhaps the problem that this creates is not immediately obvious. Consider the case of a passenger inside an open-topped car travelling at 30 metres a second or approximately 65 mph (the metric system will be used throughout because, for one thing, the speed of light is easier to express in this system). Suppose he now throws a ball forwards, at a further 30 metres a second relative to the car, in the direction of a stationary pedestrian. It will, of course, approach the unfortunate pedestrian at 60 metres per second – at least to any reasonable degree of accuracy. If, on the other hand, the passenger were to hurl it backwards towards the pedestrian at 30 metres a second it would appear stationary to this observer. The ball would still be moving backwards at 30 metres per second relative to both occupants of the car. In either case, it is going to be difficult to catch.

Now if the same passenger were to shine a light towards this pedestrian both the passenger and pedestrian would say that the light was travelling at 300 million metres a second, and not 300 million plus or minus the speed of the car, as you might expect from the above example. In fact, both passenger and pedestrian would claim that it left the car at this velocity and reached the pedestrian at this speed. And both of them would be absolutely correct. The same would be true if the experiment were performed using an aircraft or a spacecraft, and it does not matter at what speed they were moving relative to the observer, up to, and including, the speed of light.

This startling fact was first discovered in the second half of the nineteenth century by two scientists called Michelson and Morley who were attempting to measure the absolute speed of the Earth. Since this experiment heralded a turning point in our understanding of the nature of the universe, it is worth examining its basic premise and results in some detail.

The Michelson–Morley experiment

The Earth revolves around the sun. The sun also moves, revolving about the centre of the Milky Way. Similarly, the Milky Way moves within the galactic cluster to which it belongs, and, in its turn, that galactic cluster moves in some manner relative to all the other galactic clusters; and so on. Is there, then, some stationary background ether against which objects move in an absolute sense? During the last century the answer was believed to be an unequivocal yes.

Now if this is the case we can go on and sensibly ask: what is the absolute speed of the Earth relative to this stationary background? One way of measuring it would be to observe how fast we travel relative to the background of fixed stars. There are two problems here. The first is the difficulty in accurately measuring the angular shift in the apparent position of distant stellar objects over such incredible distances. The second is the possibility that the stars themselves may be hurtling along at some speed in the same direction. In either case, the value we obtain for the velocity of the Earth would be totally invalid. Consider trying to determine the speed of a train in which you were a passenger by making measurements upon a passing aircraft – it is quite possible you would come to the conclusion that you were moving backwards.

An alternative method of measuring this absolute velocity was employed by Michelson and Morley. Light, it was assumed at that time, moved at a constant velocity relative to this hypothetical ether. Michelson and Morley reasoned that, if they measured the velocity of light in two perpendicular directions, they would get different answers. In addition, if they were to perform the experiment at different times of the year they would obtain different results depending on whether the Earth's orbital motion caused it to be travelling in the same direction, or opposite to, the direction of the sun's absolute motion. The actual experimental procedure is not important in the context of this book, but interested readers can find it in most advanced physics textbooks; essentially it was all done with mirrors. The part that is of importance to us is the result. For Michelson and Morley found that the speed of light was always the same.

This was a little disturbing for the scientists of the time; as usual, rather than question the assumptions upon which they had based their experiments, they attempted to patch up the existing theory to fit the results. The ether, or so it was argued, was being dragged along with the Earth and locally we were static with respect to it. This gave rise to many new problems, such as the absence of the expected distortion of the light from distant objects as it passed through these ether ripples – an effect similar to what happens to our view of the bottom of a pond when the surface of the water is disturbed. Additionally, if the relatively small Earth could drag the ether along with it, might not also the far more massive suns and galaxies do the same? If so, the ether could no longer be considered as the universal absolute static background. What, then, was the absolute frame of reference against which all motion could be measured? The answer is: there isn't one. Motion can only be meaningfully discussed in relation to something else. In retrospect, the problem of an absolute stationary frame is difficult to express. Even in Michelson and Morley's time the problem was framed in terms of motion relative to the 'fixed' stars, or relative to the background ether.

So motion is not the absolute it was previously believed to be. It is relative, and we can only talk about a thing's motion relative to something else, not as an absolute property in isolation. Michelson and Morley's result should not be viewed as a failure. They had failed to determine the Earth's absolute velocity, yes, but they had succeeded in disproving the general idea of an absolute velocity and, in its place, established the speed of light as the new great absolute, a universal constant for all inertial observers.

In retrospect, the constancy of the velocity of light is not such a startling result as it might first appear. Consider what would happen if the converse were true – that the speed of light varied with the velocity of an object relative to the observer. The light from an object moving towards you would then move faster than the light from a stationary one. Imagine a car heading rapidly towards you colliding with another moving slowly across your line of vision. With a variable speed of light, the light from the car approaching you would reach you first. Therefore you would see the impact of the first car before that of the second. The front of the first car would crumple as it appeared to collide with nothing. Some time later you would see the second car enter the space occupied by the first and then skid sideways towards you until it came to a halt immediately in front of the first, blocking your view of it. But how could you have seen the front of the first car crumple? And how could you have seen the second one enter the space occupied by the first? The light from it would have to pass through the first car. Clearly this is absurd, but realization of the contradictions implicit in a variable speed of light came only after the development of a theory to account for Michelson and Morley's results. This theory was, of course, Einstein's special relativity.

The special theory of relativity

Einstein replaced Newton's set of equations relating the measurements of different inertial observers with:

$$x' = x$$
$$y' = y$$
$$z' = \gamma (z - v\,t)$$
$$t' = \gamma \left(t - \frac{vz}{c^2}\right)$$

where, as before, the symbol   denotes the measurements of an observer moving at a velocity v relative to one in the x, y, z, t frame,

$$\gamma = \left(1 - \frac{v^2}{c^2}\right)^{\frac{1}{2}}$$

and c is the, all-important, speed of light. These are the Lorentz transformation equations, named after the nineteenth-century Dutch mathematician who first derived them. Similarly, for the Lorentz factor.

There are several elegant proofs that these transformation equations satisfy Michelson and Morley's observation of a constant speed of light. All standard texts on special relativity contain one, and the choice of which derivation to provide is a matter of preference on the author's part; each offers slightly different insights. I shall not go into a detailed mathematical analysis of my own personal favourite here; interested readers are recommended to look at several of these texts.

Before we go on to explore the consequences of special relativity, it is worth examining some of the new features of the theory. First, the Lorentz factor does not occur in the directions in which there is no motion. Consequently, the axes are usually chosen so that one axis lies along the direction of motion; the other two spatial axes can then be ignored, which greatly simplifies the analyses. Second, as we have seen, for most everyday purposes it is so small that it is completely negligible. For example, suppose we are travelling at 10 metres per second (about 20 mph) relative to a stationary observer. The difference in our measurements from those of the stationary observer will be less than 10^{-17}, the value of the Lorentz factor at 10 metres per second. This is also the error involved in using Newton's equations, which is the reason we continue to use them and also why it took so long to realize that they were not perfectly accurate. However, in measurements involving very high speeds, or extending very large distances and over very long periods of time, the effects of the Lorentz factor manifest themselves dramatically.

The two most obvious consequences of relative motion as revealed by the Lorentz transformation are length contraction and time dilation.

Length contraction
For moving objects distance becomes contracted, or shortened, in the direction of motion, relative to a stationary observer, by an amount equal to the Lorentz factor; i.e.

$$L = \frac{L_0}{\gamma}$$

where L is the length of a moving object, in the direction of motion, and L_0 is the length of the object when it is stationary. So if you were to measure the length of a passing spacecraft, the value you obtain would be less than that measured by a passenger within it, provided both your measurements were sufficiently accurate (see Fig. 3.2). Remember that, now stationary is a relative term, the passenger will observe the same contraction in objects at rest relative to you.

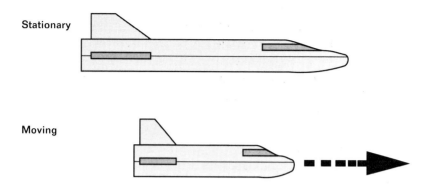

Stationary

Moving

Fig. 3.2 Length contraction: moving objects shrink in the direction of motion.

Time dilation

For moving observers, in addition to length contraction, the time taken for events to occur is greater by the same factor, i.e.

$$T = \gamma T_0$$

where T is the passage of time of a moving object, in the direction of motion, and T_0 is that of the object when it is stationary. Consequently, the watch of the passenger in the above example would appear to run slowly relative to yours (see Fig. 3.3).

Time dilation has been verified in several experiments, the most notable being those aboard the manned lunar probes. However, in the case of the astronauts, for all their travelling, the difference between their clocks and those remaining on Earth was only a few seconds.

These effects become increasingly apparent with increasing relative velocity. Furthermore, this process is not linear; that is, at low speeds it is almost negligible, but it increases ever more rapidly as we get closer to the speed of light, c (see Fig. 3.4). For example, at $\frac{1}{4}$c the Lorentz factor is 1.03, at $\frac{1}{2}$c it is 1.16, at $\frac{3}{4}$c 1.51, and as we approach the speed of light it becomes infinite. At this point a moving object would be infinitely narrow, of absolutely zero length, in the direction of motion. It would also be frozen in time. So to us, and indeed to all observers moving at less than the speed of light relative to us, the object would remain unchanging forever. This has to be so in order that the velocity

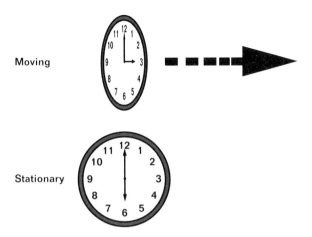

Fig. 3.3 Time dilation: moving clocks run slow.

of a beam of light leaving such an object – a spaceship, say – would appear to both us and someone on board as moving at the speed of light. For us it would never separate from the surface of the spaceship, while to someone on board it would move away at the speed of light, which can only be true if their time is at a relative standstill.

Obviously, there are several other difficulties involved with travel at the speed of light. Besides those involved with having zero length and

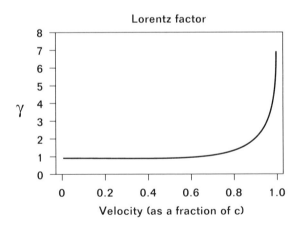

Fig. 3.4 The Lorentz factor increases non-linearly with velocity, approaching infinity as the velocity approaches that of light.

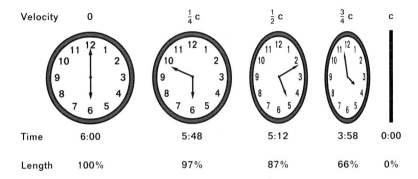

Fig. 3.5 If a set of clocks in relative motion are synchronized at twelve o'clock, six hours later (by the one at rest relative to us) they will all read differently. The amount of the difference in each case is given by the Lorentz factor.

being stationary in time, there is the problem of the increase in mass.

Mass

Before we go on to the effect of motion on mass it is worth while explaining exactly what mass is. Mass is an intrinsic property of all matter. Unfortunately, because it is closely associated with weight it is often confused with it; we even use the same units to measure the two. The difference between mass and weight lies in the difference between pushing and lifting an object. Place a pencil in a bowl of water, push it gently and it will begin to move. The effort required to push (accelerate) the pencil up to a given speed is the same here on Earth, on the moon, in space, in fact anywhere. This effort is directly related to its mass. Now lift the pencil and hold it. The effort required to hold it up against the force of gravity is its weight. On the moon this effort would only be one-sixth of the effort here on Earth, because of the reduced gravity. In orbit no effort whatsoever is required, because there is no gravity – amply demonstrated by film sequences of orbiting astronauts.

The confusion between mass and weight arises because the force of gravity is proportional to the mass. Double the mass and twice the effort is needed to support it – it has twice the weight. But weight is a local phenomenon, for it depends on what planet we are on, and vanishes altogether when we are in free space. Alternatively, mass is universal, it is constant everywhere – or, at least, rest mass is. Rest mass is the mass which an object has when it is at rest relative to us. For a moving object, mass, like distance and time, varies. In fact it increases, and, not surprisingly, by the Lorentz factor:

$$m = \gamma\, m_0$$

where m_0 is the mass at rest. Obviously, mass also increases to infinity as an object approaches the speed of light. Consequently, it gets harder and harder to accelerate something as it approaches c. Indeed, to accelerate externally any material object to the velocity of light would require an infinite amount of energy – more than there is in our universe, or for that matter in any finite universe. As a result, it is not possible to push any object with a finite rest mass, no matter how small, up to the speed of light. Light can travel at this speed only because it has zero rest mass. It is a general rule that only those things which possess zero rest mass can travel at the speed of light, and conversely such things can only exist at this speed.

As we saw earlier, mass and energy can be converted into each other. In a very real sense, they are two manifestations of the same thing. In Newton's time the mass of an object was believed to be constant for all inertial observers. Additionally, although energy could be converted from one form to another – work to heat, motion to work and so on – it could never be created or destroyed. Einstein's relativity has shown that mass is actually another form of energy, that either can be converted to the other, and that it is the total mass-energy of a system that is conserved.

The Lorentz transformation also tells us that the speed of light, c, is an upper limit to the relative velocity that anything can have. This contrasts sharply with Newtonian mechanics, in which travel at any speed is possible. It is worth noting, though, that in Newton's theory it also requires an infinite amount of energy to attain this 'infinite limiting velocity', just as it does to attain the velocity of light in Einstein's. This brings us back to the problem posed on page 34, in which we saw that if we 'add' the speed of light to that of a moving observer the result still has to be the speed of light. Obviously, the rules of addition for relativistic velocities must be different from those with which we are familiar. This is not too surprising, since measurements of both distance and time are different for different inertial observers, and it is precisely these two quantities that are used to calculate velocity. Without going into the intervening mathematics, when an observer moving at a velocity v relative to you launches an object in the same direction at a velocity he measures to be v', the combined velocity can be measured as

$$v'' = \frac{v + v}{\left(1 + \frac{v'v}{c^2}\right)}$$

and not v + v'. Substituting c for v' in this equation results in v'' = c, as required. Indeed, working backwards from this preposition is one means of deriving the Lorentz transformation equations. As a further consequence, 'adding' any two sub-light velocities will always result in a sub-light velocity. This argument immediately generalizes to any number of sub-light velocities.

Essentially, the speed of light in Einstein's theory serves the same purpose as infinite speed in Newton's. Both provide an upper bound for velocity, momentum, energy and a host of other quantities.

The phenomena that result from using the Lorentz transformation are somewhat different from those which we encounter in everyday life, but I would like to emphasize that this is only because in everyday life the effects are just too small to notice. This strangeness should not be considered in any way off-putting, but simply an exciting twist in the way in which the universe works. Unfortunately, the unfamiliarity does occasionally give rise to misunderstandings, so it is perhaps worth considering in depth some examples of the effects.

Travel within special relativity

Let us now look, in some detail, at a case where two observers are moving at a relative velocity of $\frac{3}{4}$c. For the sake of argument imagine that you are one observer and I am the other, and that we are both aboard spacecraft. Now you will observe me approaching, passing and departing from you at $\frac{3}{4}$c. Consequently I will appear only 66 per cent as long to you, in the direction of motion, as I do to myself. Also, to you things will appear to take 51 per cent longer to occur aboard my spacecraft than they do to me. Yet I am quite at liberty to make the same observations about your craft. The only difference between the equations I must use and yours would be in the sign of the velocity, as we are moving in opposite directions relative to one another. This change of sign makes no difference to either the length contraction or time dilation that I observe. So to me, it is you who look distinctly thin, and who are moving very slowly about your craft. For as far as I am concerned, it is you who are experiencing length contraction and time dilation. This should not worry either of us – it is simply part of the relative nature of the universe in which we live. And it is not only velocity that is relative. So too are all the phenomena associated with it: space, time, and a whole gamut of others that we shall be looking at later.

This probably still seems somewhat paradoxical; yes, as promised, we are back to those again. This and several other apparent paradoxes were used as early objections to Einstein's special relativity. Perhaps the most famous of these is the 'twin paradox', and by now, you should not be surprised if the analysis of this paradox results in a better understanding of relativity.

The twin paradox

The special theory of relativity predicts that if one of a pair of twins is sent off into space in a spacecraft, on his return he will find his brother much older. This is not the paradox, but simply an example of time dilation. The paradox arises as follows. Suppose both twins are placed in rockets that are then driven rapidly apart. We will assume tha both are familiar with Einstein's theory. Consequently one – let's call him Cain – can reason that since his brother Abel is moving rapidly relative to Cain, then it is Abel who will age less rapidly. Abel can reason equally well and comes to the same conclusion about Cain – that it is Cain who will age less rapidly. And so we have our paradox.

What does Einstein's theory say the brothers will find when they are brought back together again? Well, it depends entirely on the way in which the bringing back is done – more precisely, on which of the brothers experiences the necessary accelerations to bring him to rest near his brother. If Cain undergoes all the necessary velocity changes, then it is he who will benefit from the reduced passage of time; similarly for Abel, if it is he who undergoes all the accelerations. And if both experience the same accelerations to get back together again, then they will be the same age when they meet. They will, as it were, have caught up with lost time – or at least each other's. Someone who had remained at the original point of departure, and final meeting point, of the two brothers would have aged more than both.

So much for the paradox. Like those of Chapter 1, it has vanished before the light of complete understanding, and in the process we have learnt some valuable lessons.

In general, the resolution of all problems of this kind associated with special relativity depends entirely upon who experiences the necessary accelerations. Fortunately, special relativity provides a recipe for taking these factors into account, and for allowing the brothers, and any other interested observer, to calculate the results of any measurement that either brother might make. Space, too, is affected in the same manner and degree as time, although in the opposite sense. It is fortunate indeed that special relativity exists to act as arbitrator; otherwise the two brothers might well be moved to violence over the disparity in the distance covered and age attained which each ascribes to the other!

Relativistic travel

As another illustration of exactly what it means to live in our relativistic universe, I would like to send you on a short imaginary journey – short at least in terms of interstellar space – to the nearest of our neighbouring stars, Proxima Centauri, and back. By human standards such a journey is actually quite a long one; it is certainly longer than any yet undertaken by man, or even our machines, the unmanned Voyagers, that have explored some of the outer planets. Although these machines have now been under way for many years and have achieved some of the fastest (relative) speeds attained by man-made objects, they have yet to reach the outer limits of our solar system. (I give this information only as an example of the difference between what we can achieve and what is necessary if we hope to undertake the following journey of the mind.)

We will assume, for convenience, that you are already moving at three-quarters the speed of light. I, the other observer, will remain here on Earth. Now Proxima Centauri is approximately 4 light years from Earth, at least when I measure it. Therefore, at your speed it will take you $5\frac{1}{3}$ years of my time to travel each way. We will ignore all problems associated with turning around to come back. Now Lorentz time dilation causes time to run more slowly for you than for me. Consequently, you measure only $3\frac{1}{2}$ years for each half of the journey. But if you have covered 4 light years in less than 4 years, does this mean that you have travelled faster than the speed of light? The answer is no! For you, Lorentz length contraction reduces the distance between the Earth and Proxima Centauri to only 2.6 light years, which at a velocity of $\frac{3}{4}c$ you would indeed cover in $3\frac{1}{2}$ years. Conversely, I account for this by the reduced passage of time you experience. As for when you get back, we will both agree that it is you who have aged less, as it is you who have undergone the all-important accelerations and decelerations involved in the journey.

Having made the point that you do not at any time travel faster than the speed of light, it is still interesting to note that, neglecting the problems of acceleration, starting from rest on Earth you would have succeeded in covering the 4 light years in $3\frac{1}{2}$ years. The shrinking of the distance for you would have occurred during the acceleration. The closer to the speed of light you travel, the better off you are by far in terms of how quickly you can cover distance. For this is not a linear relationship. Go fast enough and you could cross the 100,000 light years of our galaxy in the space of a lifetime, or less. At the speed of light you could cross the entire universe in no time at all, at least as you measure time. This is what was meant above when it was noted that the speed of light serves the same function in Einstein's relativity that an infinite speed does in Newton's. This compensates for the extra effort it takes to accelerate an object in Einsteinian mechanics, and why an infinite energy is required to accelerate something to the speed of light.

Essentially, things have not really changed that much in going from Newton's to Einstein's relativity – at least as far as the interstellar traveller is concerned. However, when he returns to Earth he will find that a lot more time has passed than Newton would have expected. The only other difference is the added complication in solving problems in Einsteinian mechanics; but as we have seen, for most everyday purposes Newtonian mechanics are perfectly adequate. When Einstein's equations are essential, the advent of the pocket calculator and personal computer makes the calculations no more difficult for us than those necessitated by Newton's were for our forefathers.

The fourth dimension

As we have seen, neither space, time, mass nor various other quantities with which we are familiar remain constant in Einstein's relativity. Yet there are certain quantities that do. All these new invariants are related to four-dimensional quantities and not three, such as distance, or one, such as time and mass. For example, Newton's three-space distance d, between two points, is given by:

$$d = (\Delta x^2 + \Delta y^2 + \Delta z^2)^{\frac{1}{2}}$$

where Δx, Δy, Δz are the lengths, or more correctly the difference in the coordinates, in each of the three spatial directions. This distance remains constant for fixed displacements of the origin (translations), for rotations of the coordinate axes and in Newtonian mechanics for moving observers. Draw a 3-inch line on a piece of graph paper parallel to the horizontal axis Now move it to the left. The line remains unchanged in length. Now rotate it. The lengths in the x and y directions, Δx and Δy, will change but its total length, d, will not. The distance d, in Newton's three-space, is said to be invariant with respect to these transformations.

In Einstein's relativity the three-distance, d, is still invariant with respect to displacement and rotation, but not with respect to motion. For a moving object, at least one of the lengths from which the distance, d, is calculated is contracted relative to a stationary observer. Although you could not measure it for any achievable speed, the 3-inch line above would shrink a little when in motion. Similarly, a watch attached to the moving line would run more slowly.

In Einsteinian four-space, the equivalence of three-space distance is

$$s = (\Delta x^2 + \Delta y^2 + \Delta z^2 - (c.\Delta t)^2)^{\frac{1}{2}}$$
$$= (d^2 - c.\Delta t^2)^{\frac{1}{2}}$$

and this new distance, s, does indeed remain constant for all observers who are in relative motion; in other words, no matter what individual values they measure for each of the components Δx, Δy, Δz and Δt, the value they calculate for s is the same for all. A simple substitution of these values for those of a moving observer given by the Lorentz transformation is all that is necessary to confirm this. In every case, the contraction of length is exactly balanced by the dilation of time. This new four-space quantity really is just like three-space distance except for the inclusion of time. The factor c, the speed of light, serves simply to convert the units of time into those of distance. The negative sign of the temporal component allows four-distances to have both positive and negative values. In contrast, classical three-distance could never be negative. This has several interesting consequences, one of which is that all sub-light four-distances have the same sign, negative.

The above four-distance, s, is said to be a Lorentz transformation invariant and has the same value for all inertial observers. Similarly, the three-distance, d, is invariant with respect to the transformation equations of Newton. Invariants play an important role in characterizing the nature of space-time. In general, all four-space quantities or vectors – four-velocity, four-acceleration, four-momentum and so on –

are invariants. These four-vectors are also characterized by one squared quantity having the opposite sign to the other three (see Appendix A). Not at all surprisingly, the one 'odd man out' in all of them involves the temporal component.

Collectively, the signs of the components that combine to form invariants are termed the signature. The signature of our Einsteinian universe is $(+++-)$, and that of the Newtonian one $(+++)$. (Note that some textbooks adopt a convention in which the signature is $(---+)$ for four-vectors.) This results in four-distances being positive for all sub-light inertial observers. The choice of which convention to adopt is completely arbitrary and does not affect any of the properties of the space, or the arguments within this book.

All the laws of physics are far more accurately described by this new four-dimensional representation. This is the reason why we say the universe is four- and not three-dimensional – an important point and one that cannot be dismissed lightly. With the necessity of accepting the Lorentz transformation, space and time become inextricably bound together. Treating them as entirely separate entities is an approximation – that of Newton's relativity; although, as we have seen, for everyday problems such as how long will it take me to get from London to Edinburgh at 80 kilometres per hour this approximation is perfectly adequate. Errors in our measurement, and the inevitable traffic hold-ups, will far outweigh those associated with the inaccuracies of Newton's equations.

Let us return now to consideration of the opposite sign of one quantity in all four-vectors. Without this the four-vectors would look exactly like the three-vectors with which we are familiar, with one additional component. In such a system four-distance would be

$$s = (\Delta x^2 + \Delta y^2 + \Delta z^2 + \Delta T^2)^{\frac{1}{2}}$$

The nineteenth-century Russian scientist Minkowski reasoned in exactly this way.

The Minkowski representation
Minkowski proposed that four-vectors should have the form $(\alpha, \beta, \delta, ic\epsilon)$, where i is the square root of -1. Introducing i has the desired effect of allowing us to add this quantity to the others when we square; as the i^2 term automatically introduces the minus sign. Again, the constant c is necessary so that all components of the four-vectors

are in the same units. The position of a particle in space-time is then (x, y, z, ict), with each component having the same units of distance. The Lorentz transformation for space-time is now

$$x = x'$$
$$y = y'$$
$$z = (z' - v\,t')$$
$$ict = ic\left(t' - \frac{z'v}{c^2}\right)$$

Substituting ΔT ($=ic\Delta t$) into the equation before this one results in a distance composed of entirely positive quantities. This incorporation of 'i' into the four vectors replaces signature in the 'real' representation. The advantages of using this new representation will become apparent later.

Travel in an Einsteinian v. a Newtonian universe

Einsteinian relativity has one surprising advantage over Newtonian. As we have seen, it permits us to travel to any point in the universe and back in a single lifetime. This may seem an extraordinary statement, for in Newtonian mechanics we can travel at any speed, while in Einsteinian the fastest speed we are able to travel is that of light, 300 million metres per second. Yet even at this speed it takes light 2 million years to reach Andromeda, our nearest neighbouring galaxy; if we could travel at infinite speeds we would reach it in no time at all! Unfortunately, we have neglected to take into account the time and energy required to reach these speeds.

To change the velocity of anything we must accelerate it. This involves doing work in some fashion. For example, to get a car to 30 kilometres per hour from rest the engine must burn petrol. Once it has reached this speed we have to do additional work to maintain that speed in order to overcome the forces of air resistance and internal friction. In the case of a spaceship, the absence of matter in vacuum, and of moving parts, results in it continuing onwards at whatever speed we have imparted to it during acceleration. The unmanned probes that were launched over the last two decades were accelerated for short times only. Essentially, these probes now drift at the velocity they possessed when their rockets were switched off many years ago, neglecting the effects of gravity. And they will continue to do so for many, many years to come.

Let's now take an imaginary journey to Andromeda, some 2 million light years away. For the time being we will ignore the problems of propulsion and allow our imagination free rein. First, we shall take this journey in a Newtonian universe. For simplicity we will assume that the effects of friction and gravity are negligible. How fast do we wish to accelerate? Well, if we could accelerate at an infinite rate we could reach an infinite speed instantly, and reach our destination in no time at all. Unfortunately, if we were to do so we would experience infinite acceleration forces, and be crushed to an infinitesimally thin film instantly! What then should our rate of acceleration be? At this moment your body is being subjected to a force equivalent to an acceleration of 9.81 m/s^2. It has been for the entire time you have been reading this book – at least I assume it has, provided you are on the planet Earth and subject to its gravitational field of 1 g, 9.81 m/s^2. Consequently, this would be a comfortable acceleration to subject us to.

Naturally, the greater the acceleration the sooner we get to our destination. Yet to stand in a 2 g field is equivalent to having someone of your own weight perched on your shoulders. Additionally, the blood would be pulled to your lower body, causing you to pass out, and falling in a 2 g field is not a very pleasant prospect. Quite apart from the extra weight, you also fall faster. The high g forces to which astronauts and test pilots are subjected last for short periods only, and they are obliged to lie on their backs throughout the experience. For the sake of argument then, we shall stick with a comfortable acceleration of 1 g.

So how long to Andromeda at 9.81 m/s^2 using Newton's theory? We will add the condition that we wish to stop when we get there, if only to turn around and come back. The best time we can make is achieved by accelerating for the first half of the journey and decelerating for the second. The total time for the trip is then some 2800 years.

Consider the same journey in our Einsteinian universe. Now we are limited to the speed of light, a speed we would reach at 1 g in 3×10^7 seconds, or a little under 354 days; let's say a year. After we reach this speed, how much longer will it take to reach Andromeda? The answer is no time at all, for the distance to Andromeda will have shrunk to zero for the spacecraft. We are discussing here proper time – the time experienced by those of us on board the spaceship. To the people back on Earth a considerable length of time would pass; 2 million years even if we neglect the additional time involved in accelerating. But for now we are only concerned with our own travelling and will ignore the opinion of those we have left behind. For us, the faster we move, the shorter the distance to our destination becomes and the quicker we get there.

For practical reasons, such as having no way of navigating in an infinitely thin universe, we would stop just short of the speed of light at the halfway point and reverse engines to come to a halt in Andromeda. The entire trip would then have taken a little less than two years at a comfortable 1 g. The same is true of a trip to anywhere within the universe. We can get literally anywhere in a little under two years; four for the round trip.

There is also the question of power. For the Newtonian case the power requirement is enormous, even assuming perfect efficiency; I leave its calculation up to the interested reader. In our Einsteinian universe the power is large, though considerably less than in the Newtonian one. In fact, to get us up to the speed of light requires an amount of energy equal to the rest mass energy of our craft. And this same amount of energy will get us absolutely anywhere!

Earlier I mentioned that it would take an infinite amount of energy externally to accelerate an object to the speed of light. I was also careful to say 'externally accelerate'. For this is necessary to provide the extra energy required for the increase in mass associated with the increased speed. When the acceleration is generated from within, by using rocket engines for instance, the total mass-energy must remain constant. Now if we could somehow convert half the rest mass of a spacecraft into pure energy, and project all of this behind us slowly so that it accelerated at 1 g, the remainder of our craft would reach the speed of light – albeit in an infinite time from the point of view of an unaccelerated (inertial) observer. To them, our actions would become slower and slower as we accelerated, and each additional metre per second of speed would take us longer to achieve. We, of course, would be unaware of this.

In practice there would be the problems of payload v. total mass, efficiency and how to construct the engines. So far, on mankind's real journeying in space, we have had to be satisfied with barely escaping the gravitational field of the Earth and then drifting slowly to the moon, with all its concomitant problems of free fall. People, it seems, are built for 1 g; increase this force and we experience the problems outlined above; decrease it, and our muscles and bones rapidly waste away. This is why rotating spacecraft and space stations have been proposed – to provide an artificial gravity. As we have seen, a better solution, if we could achieve it, would be to maintain a constant acceleration of 1 g towards our destination for the first half of our journey, and then a constant deceleration of 1 g for the second half.

There is also the problem of the friction associated with our speed. The impact of matter on the outer shell of the spacecraft will both slow it down and heat it. Though space is ostensibly empty, with increasing speed the little matter that there is would become increasingly concentrated. In addition, its relative mass increases and it becomes more concentrated in the direction of motion, due to the contraction of length. Consequently, we would encounter it with ever greater frequency. Indeed, as we approach the speed of light the whole universe becomes concentrated into an infinitely thin, and consequently infinitely dense, barrier in the direction in which we are travelling. The force of friction would increase accordingly.

The problems associated with producing sufficient acceleration while overcoming the ever-increasing force of friction are essentially technological, and I would be the last person to admit that anything is impossible on technological grounds alone. Too many scientists of the past who have objected on these grounds have subsequently been proven wrong.

There remain also the problems associated with time dilation – or perhaps difficulties would be more accurate. Our trip to Andromeda would be exciting, but to whom would we tell the tale of our journey when we returned? In something over 4 million years, one or two changes would have undoubtedly taken place back here on Earth. This would seem to be an insurmountable drawback, and one which will be discussed at some length later. At the very least, in our Einsteinian universe, we would have survived the journey – which is considerably better than the situation in a Newtonian one.

In this chapter we have only scratched the surface of the evidence for, and the consequences of, Einstein's rather than Newton's relativity. The full weight of this evidence is overwhelming, and the consequences extremely far-reaching. From now on we will take it for granted that this new relativity of Einstein is accurate.

· IV ·

Distance v. Time: The Fourth Dimension

Clearly, any real body must have extension in four directions: it must have, Length, Breadth, Thickness and Duration. But through a natural infirmity of the flesh, which I explain to you in a moment, we incline to overlook this fact. There are really four dimensions, three, which we call the three planes of Space, and a fourth, Time. There is, however, a tendency to draw an unreal distinction between the former three dimensions and the latter, because it happens our consciousness moves intermittently in one direction along the latter from the beginning to the end of our lives.

H.G. Wells, *The Time Machine*
(published in 1895, ten years before Einstein's *Special Theory of Relativity*)

In Chapter 3 we touched upon four-dimensionality. This is a difficult concept, and one that deserves careful examination. One thing this chapter will not do is enable you to envisage a fourth dimension. I cannot envisage four dimensions, no one I have ever met can envisage four dimensions, and anyone who claims they can should be viewed with great trepidation! We evolved with our present capabilities to cope with the universe of our everyday experience, and we simply do not have the ability directly to observe, or imagine, four dimensions. How then can we, or for that matter anyone, hope to handle this idea?

The answer is that we can do it indirectly, by analogy. We will begin the process by losing a few dimensions, in order to work with ideas with which we are familiar. Once we have developed the rules for one, two and three dimensions, we will generalize them to higher dimensions. For example, you know how to add one-dimensional numbers: $1 + 2 = 3$. It may surprise you to learn that you also know how to add two-dimensional numbers. Walk 3 paces north and 2 paces east. Then take 5 more north and 4 more east. Where are you relative to your starting position? The answer is obviously 8 paces north and 6 east from where you started – at least on a flat surface. On the surface of the Earth this would not be strictly true, as you would have to take account of the curvature. But for now we will content ourselves with flat, Euclidean spaces and leave curvature until later.

What exactly did you do to arrive at the result above? You added the paces to the north and those to the east independently: $(3, 2) + (5, 4) = (8, 6)$. This is reasonable – movement north is independent of movement east, and vice versa. It is also reasonable to expect this independence to hold true for any number of dimensions. This gives us a means of generalizing the rule for addition of vectors (x, y) in two dimensions, to higher ones: add the components term by term. To incorporate a third dimension, height, simply insert a third coordinate into our vector to give (x, y, z), and we already have the rule for addition. We can now reason by analogy to obtain a four-dimensional space (x, y, z, f), f standing for fourth. Again we already know the rule for adding two such four-vectors, term by term independently.

The general rule for subtraction of vectors with any number of dimensions follows immediately. The same is true for all vector manipulations. This is the basis of the formal mathematical approach for dealing with four and higher numbers of dimensions.

There is also another extremely useful technique we can employ when trying to understand higher dimensions. Similar in principle to the formal mathematical approach above, it involves shedding dimensions and arguing by analogy. This alternative approach involves imagining a two-dimensional universe inhabited by intelligent analogues of ourselves, 'flatlanders'. Strictly this is a three-space-time universe, since flatlanders need a temporal dimension in which to exist just as we do, but this does not affect any of the present arguments.

Flatlanders

Our flatlanders exist entirely within a two dimensional universe and encounter only two-dimensional objects. They 'see' these objects with a two-dimensional equivalent of light that is also confined to the surface of their universe. Flatlanders cannot move off the surface of flatland – from their point of view there is nowhere to move off to. Flatlanders can no more directly imagine a third dimension than we can a fourth.

Appreciation of the difficulties that flatlanders have in dealing with the idea of a three-dimensional space enables us to understand our own limitations regarding four-space. It also provides us with insights into how we might overcome these limitations. For example, flatlanders encounter only the edges of objects in their universe, just as we encounter only the outer surface of things. For them to be able to 'see' a surface would be analogous to our seeing the whole internal volume of an object. This is different from seeing through something. For example, modern medical science can obtain complete three-dimensional scans of the human body. To view these data they have to be presented as a series of sections, flat surface slices or angled cuts into a normal surface picture. Attempts to display semi-transparent views of interior structure, like those of the children's educational toy the Invisible Man, fall a long way short of true three-dimensionality. The fault lies not with the information or our ability to display it, but with our psychological inability to interpret full three-dimensional information. Sight functions by the reflection of light from surfaces. We simply do not have a sense for perceiving true three-dimensionality.

We can look down on flatland and see inside the edges of objects, but this is because we exist in three dimensions. When we look down on flatland like this we are doing the equivalent of a four-dimensional observer gazing at our volumes. Perhaps we should not be too embarrassed by our inability to interpret complete three-dimensional information, but instead be proud of how well we deal with what is essentially a four-dimensional view.

Now flatlanders could deduce the addition rule for higher dimensions, much as we ourselves did above. We have the advantage that any general rule we hypothesize from a two-dimensional model we can test in three dimensions – again, just as we did above. Similarly, flatlanders could deduce other properties of three-space, such as spatial distance. Returning to our earlier example of walking north and east, after our two bouts of walking we finished a total distance of 10 paces (= $(8^2 + 6^2)^{\frac{1}{2}}$) from our starting point. Restricting ourselves, and the flatlanders, to 'flat', Euclidean spaces, from the above formula for distance the flatlanders might argue that, in three dimensions, distance is determined by taking the square root of the sum of all three coordinate distances squared. This, as we know, is correct. In just the same way, we can deduce the form of four-space distance. However, as we saw in Chapter 3, when the dimension is time we must introduce i into the definition of the fourth coordinate for the rule to work.

Curved spaces

We can learn a great deal from flatlanders. They provide us with an intuitive insight into the meaning of the formal mathematics, and point the way for further developments. They also provide a means of studying curvature in higher dimensions, since we can embed their universe in the surface of a curved three-dimensional object. For simplicity, let us choose the surface of a sphere. A sphere is useful for several reasons: it is the same everywhere; it has a finite area, two-space volume; and yet it is unbounded – there is no end to the surface. Our friendly flatlander, then, could cover every part of this surface and yet never encounter an edge or boundary of any kind.

Now if the radius of the sphere is large enough, it would be difficult for a flatlander to distinguish it from a flat plane, in the same way as it was difficult for our ancestors to discover the curvature of the Earth. So how might he go about measuring the curvature? Well, in Euclidean space the angles of a triangle add up to 180°. This is not so in curved spaces. To see this, take a ball and draw on the surface of it a line extending one quarter of the way around the circumference. Our flatlander on the surface of a sphere would consider this a straight line, which, in his two-dimensional universe, it is. Now turn through 90° anticlockwise and draw a second 'straight' line, again of one-quarter the circumference. Turn again through 90° anticlockwise and draw a third straight line of the same length. If you have done this correctly you should be back at the start and this third line should join the first at right angles (see Fig. 4.1).

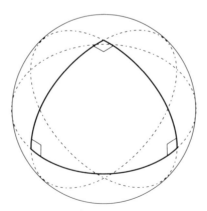

Fig. 4.1 Triangle embedded in the surface of a sphere.

From our flatlander's point of view we have drawn a triangle. If we add up the three angles of 90° we arrive at the answer of 270° for the sum of the angles of our triangle.

Do all triangles drawn on a sphere add up to 270°? The answer is no. If the triangle is very small compared to the size of our sphere, the sum of the internal angles of the triangle will be almost exactly 180°. As the sides of the triangle increase, the larger this sum becomes. The important point is that all these triangles on a sphere have internal angles that add up to more than 180°. In general, for any curved space the internal angles of a triangle add up to other than 180°.

In the sphere in our example above, triangles of the same size anywhere will always give the same total internal angle. If we had used an ellipsoid instead, this value would vary for similar triangles at different places on the surface, but the sum would still be greater than 180°. This last statement is true for all surfaces with positive curvature. A flat plane has zero curvature and the sum is 180°. There is a third set of surfaces for which the curvature is negative, and, not at all surprisingly, the sum of the internal angles of any triangle drawn on these surfaces is always less than 180°.

These properties are not unique to triangles. Circles drawn on curved two-dimensional surfaces have circumferences other than 2π times the radius. For our sphere, if the radius is a quarter of the sphere's circumference the resulting circle will also be a circumference of the sphere – in other words, this circumference will be four times the radius. Just as we did for the triangles, we can deduce the general rule that for all surfaces of positive curvature the ratio of the circumference to the radius will be less than 2π, and for surfaces of negative curvature greater than 2π.

It is possible, then, for our flatlander to determine whether his universe is flat or curved, provided he can make measurements of sufficient precision or over a large enough area. If the flatlander can determine the curvature of his two-dimensional universe, then we should be able to determine that of our three-dimensional one. We will have to modify the above experiments to take into account three dimensions, but that should not be too difficult. For a circle in flatland substitute a sphere in three-space, and for the circumference substitute the surface area. For the surface of a sphere in a flat Euclidean three-space, the ratio of the surface area to the radius squared is 4π. If our universe is positively curved the ratio will be less than this, and if negative more. In theory, then, we can determine the curvature of our universe, or, at the very least, whether it is positively or negatively curved. In practice, our universe is too big for us to make the necessary measurements with the required degree of precision, and local variations in the curvature might make even the determination of its sign unreliable.

As we saw in Chapter 2, there are good theoretical reasons to suppose that our universe is positively curved, that it is finite but unbounded. In later chapters we shall encounter further physical evidence for this. As we have seen, the simplest model to deal with is the uniform sphere. Lacking any reason to go to more complex curvatures, we will stay with this one.

If our familiar three-space universe is curved then it must be four-dimensional, in agreement with our arguments concerning space-time. Why, then, is time so different from space, or at least why do we perceive time as different? We have already touched upon the answers to this. In order to express time in compatible units as distance, we have to express it as ict. And it is in the presence of the square root of −1, and of the velocity of light, that the answers to this question lie.

Real imaginary numbers

The introduction of the unit imaginary number i creates conceptual problems for some people. The term 'imaginary' for numbers involving the square root of −1 (as opposed to 'real', for others) is misleading. Imaginary numbers are just as real as real ones. They are a mathematical convenience, just as using the decimal system is; imagine doing division with roman numerals, and you will appreciate the difficulties the Romans had. But 'imaginary' numbers are more than this: they are absolutely essential to mathematics. They fill a void, enabling the solution of a whole class of problems, an example of which is $(x^2+1)=0$. The idea of expressing the square root of −1 in terms of 'real' numbers is analogous to trying to express the north coordinate of position in terms of the eastern direction: the units are the same, but the directions are different. The two coordinates are said to be orthogonal – mutually inexpressible in terms of each other. The only difference between real and imaginary numbers is that when we square them we obtain quantities of opposite sign. This, as we saw in the last chapter, is precisely where the importance of i lies. It has others, too.

The use of i in the expression for time does not make the time coordinate any less real than the spatial ones. In fact, had we used the alternative signature (− − − +) for four vectors, it would be the spatial components that were imaginary and the temporal one that was real. The use of i simply introduces the correct sign when working with four-space transform invariants.

Astute readers may have noticed that the definition of four-space distance given in Chapter 3 invariably results in an imaginary value for distance for all sub-light velocities. To see this it is only necessary to substitute $(v\Delta t)^2$ for d, the spatial distance travelled by an observer in constant motion at speed v. This gives

$$\frac{s}{\Delta t} = (v^2 - c^2)^{\frac{1}{2}}$$

Four-distance s then, is an imaginary quantity and as such is more akin to the four-coordinate, time, than to the three spatial ones. There is nothing to stop us defining s in the following alternative way (equivalent to adopting the alternative signature):

$$s = (\,(c\,\Delta t)^2 - \Delta x^2 - \Delta y^2 - \Delta z^2\,)^{\frac{1}{2}}$$

Under this convention the equation is always positive; both definitions are used in different textbooks. s is then always real for sub-light speeds, though now it is necessary to express coordinates as (i Δx, i Δy, i Δz, ct), in Minkowskian form, to satisfy the above relationship. The three-space coordinate would be no more 'imaginary' than before, and the time coordinate no more 'real'. All we have done is rotate our coordinate system through a right-angle, though this is easier to see if we drop the two spatial coordinates, x and y. The reason I chose the imaginary definition of s was simply to enable me to write fewer i's in the coordinates, transforms and so on. It really makes that little difference. Whichever signature we adopt, the quantity s has the same form (real or imaginary) as the time coordinate.

Proper time
From the above arguments it would seem sensible to convert s to units of time. This is achieved simply by dividing the equation for the four-distance s by the conversion factor c throughout. This gives (after a little rearranging):

$$\tau = \left(1 - \frac{v^2}{c^2}\right)^{\frac{1}{2}} \Delta t$$
$$= \gamma\,\Delta t$$

This is just the Lorentz time dilation equation for the time measured by a moving observer. Remember, this was not how we defined it. We defined it as the Lorentz invariant, four-dimensional equivalent of distance, expressed in units of time. This, as we have seen, is the time measured by an observer moving along with the object in motion. Not surprisingly, this particular time is of fundamental importance. It is this time that must be used to derive the Lorentz invariant four-velocity, four-acceleration and so on. For these reasons this time is called the 'proper time'. In this derivation, the proper time is a natural result of adopting the Minkowskian representation of four-vectors. Introducing the quantity i may be just a mathematical convenience, but as we have seen it is a very powerful one that yields fundamental relationships between 'real' physical quantities.

We are back, then, to a physical quantity of time that in a sense is absolute, in that all observers agree upon it. Now, though, it is the proper time, the time measured in the stationary frame (that which is attached to the moving object). Though proper time is intrinsically four-dimensional, we are not so far removed from our old Newtonian notion of time. In the stationary frame the distances Δx, Δy and Δz are zero, and proper time is the same as Newton's absolute time. So four-dimensionality is not as difficult to handle as might first have been thought.

So far in this chapter we have been discussing the difference between space and time, but, as we have seen, this difference lies only in the incorporation of the fundamentally useful i into one of these 'two' types of entity. So are they really different? Well, the mathematical laws that underlie our understanding of physics imply that space and time are the same in all but this one regard. Is this factor of i enough to account for why our everyday experiences tell us that they are different? Perhaps, but there is also another reason why time is so strange, and that has to do with scale.

'c': the difference in size between space and time

You are bigger than an ant, the Earth is bigger than you. If an ant were suddenly to mutate to your size it would die. Its legs would break under the strain and its respiratory system could not cope with the mass of its body. If you were the size of a microbe you would be thrown about by the random bombardment of air molecules and would consequently be battered to death in a fraction of a second. The point of these examples is that there are excellent physical reasons for things being the size they are. Fundamental particles – electrons, protons, neutrons and so on – are of fundamental sizes. The orbits of electrons about nuclei are nothing like the orbits of planets in the solar system. Electrons can only orbit at very specific distances, given by simple numerical relationships; but more of this later. Planetary bodies can orbit at any distance. At the very small distances within the atom, quantum effects become all-important, and gravitation is extremely weak. At planetary scales quantum forces are negligible and gravity is the master of all. Scale is absolute, not relative.

Now if we look at the difference in scale between our measure of time and that of space we find they are incredibly disparate. For example, our average lifespan is seventy years while our average height is something less than 2 metres, or only 10^{-8} of a light second in the same units. The distance between one second and the next is 300 million metres, the speed of light; consequently, our average lifespan is 6.6×10^{17} metres. No one can imagine such a distance. The only reason we can handle it at all is that we have developed a versatile system of mathematics capable of handling numbers of any size.

It is this disparity in scale that accounts for a large part of our incapacity to comprehend time, the reason for our viewing it as different from space and the awe with which we regard it in general. Time is simply too large for us tiny (10^{-8} time seconds tall) humans to appreciate in the way we can distance.

If we ignore both the disparity between the sizes of time and space, on the scale of us tiny human beings, and the factor i, then the dimension of time really is exactly the same as space. And space-time really does form the four-dimensional continuum in which we live.

· V ·

FTL

To boldly go where no man has gone before!

Captain James T. Kirk of the USS *Enterprise* in *Star Trek*

FTL is the science fiction writer's stock abbreviation for Faster Than Light. It is the method by which a spacecraft can get from one star system to another in the lifetime of the crew and back again in time for tea. Well, maybe not for tea, but at least in a time that is the same as that experienced by those left behind on Earth. It makes it possible to leave Earth, flit over to Proxima Centauri in a couple of days, spend a fortnight there, take two days on the return journey, and be back on Earth eighteen or so days later.

As we saw in Chapter 4, you could indeed get to Proxima Centauri in a day or two, without the need to exceed the velocity of light, provided that you travelled at a velocity sufficiently close to c and could neglect all the problems involved in getting up to that speed. Then, after your stay, you could return inside the eighteen-day schedule outlined above – at least in principle. Unfortunately, such are the rules of sub-light travel that to cover the distance, 4 light years there and 4 back, you must have taken at least 8 Earth years. So when you get back you are in for a few shocks: your job has been taken by someone else; your children have grown up; and in your long absence your husband or wife has divorced you on the grounds of desertion and remarried. It is all very well claiming you have only been away for a few days – everyone on Earth will swear you have been away for eight years, which indeed you have.

So the idea of travelling from world to world, having strange and exotic adventures with even more strange and exotic creatures, and then dropping back later for the odd chat about old times, is just not on. The old times would be just too old for those left behind to survive the wait. And the example above is for our nearest neighbour. The galaxy is, after all, about 80,000 light years across, and this immediately converts to a minimum travel time of 80,000 Earth years. So travel as we know it is just not possible. Sailing off across the depths of space on five-year missions is all very well, but whose five years? Obviously sub-light travel puts severe restrictions on what we can reasonably expect to do. But what of travel at FTL?

FTL offers the hope of a way around these temporal limitations. It is the mechanism by which we can re-establish the absolute time that approximates so well here on Earth. As a literary device there is nothing at all wrong with FTL, but as an accurate depiction of life in an intergalactic culture there are some problems. It is a shame to dispel these illusions, but the universe is as it is. So that about wraps it up for FTL – or does it?

Special relativity tells us that it is impossible for us externally to accelerate a solid object up to the speed of light, because this requires an infinite amount of energy. This is true for a spacecraft, you, or even something as small as an electron – anything, in fact, that has a finite rest mass. For, as we impart energy to an object, its mass increases at an ever-increasing rate. But this is true only if we try to 'push' the object from the outside. If, alternatively, we somehow power the object from within, there can be no such associated increase in mass, for mass-energy cannot be created.

Consider what would happen if we could somehow convert half a spacecraft's initial mass into pure energy and eject it all in one direction – slowly, of course, so that we accelerated at 1 g. Then, by conservation of momentum, the craft would be travelling at the speed of light. As we saw in Chapter 3, this would take a little under a year to those on board the spacecraft; a year of proper time. For the rest of the universe it would quite literally take forever. Equivalently, for those on board the spacecraft, the universe would become infinitely thin in the direction of travel. And all time would pass while they were getting up to speed. Problems such as those presented by the frictional resistance of the entire universe we will ignore, since this is an ideal case in which we are concerned only with the relativistic, and not the practical, problems. Once the speed of light has been attained there is nothing to prevent the craft continuing to accelerate, and going FTL.

In special relativity, once we are travelling FTL all the troublesome infinities disappear. This fact is one that many people very quickly realize when they are first introduced to special relativity; frequently they go on to develop the mechanics of FTL objects, along with speculating on the opportunities that this offers. Generally, at this point they discover that the mathematics involves the square root of −1 (i), and promptly file all their calculations in the nearest waste basket. For, unfortunately, the Lorentz transformation is usually first introduced as a set of real equations, as it was in Chapter 3. Yet, as we saw earlier, there are excellent reasons for using the form in which i is an intrinsic part of the temporal term. So if imaginary numbers are already an integral part of the Lorentz transformation, then its reappearance in connection with FTL is certainly no reason for rejecting FTL.

Accepting the possibility of FTL leaves us with the problem of how to interpret the imaginary nature of FTL objects. One way of dealing with this, and one that has been adopted in the past, is simply to ignore the factor i for FTL velocities. This has led to the search for FTL particles; or rather, to the search for the Cherenkov radiation that would indicate the passage of an FTL particle through normal matter.

Cherenkov radiation

Named after Pavel Cherenkov, its discoverer, Cherenkov radiation is the wake that trails behind a particle when it travels through matter faster than the speed of light. It is similar to the wake you create when you move your finger through water. And just as when you move your finger faster than the speed of waves in water, the wake forms an acute angle (see Fig. 5.1)

Now Cherenkov radiation is an observed fact, though not from FTL particles; for light slows down when it passes through matter. This should not be too surprising, for light is affected by gravity and, when it

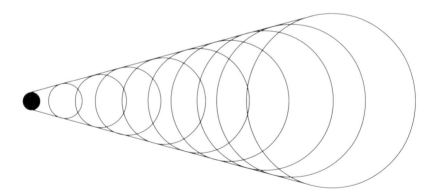

Fig. 5.1 Ripples in water. The acute angle of the wake indicates movement faster than waves in water.

passes through matter, such as air or water, it is in very close proximity to a great deal of mass. This slowing of light is the cause of refraction, the 'bending' of light by glass and water. For water the reduction in the speed of light is approximately 33 per cent, and even air slows it down by 0.03 per cent. It is possible, then, for particles of sufficiently high energy, such as cosmic rays and those generated in accelerators here on Earth, to exceed this speed. When these particles pass through matter they produce the characteristic wake of Cherenkov radiation. At no time, however, do they exceed the speed of light in vacuum, the all-important quantity in Einstein's theory. For many years researchers have sought a Cherenkov wake that is so acute that it must have come from a true FTL particle. Occasional claims have been made that a track of this kind has been found, but it has always proved to be a false alarm. I will go one stage further and, on the basis of the theories presented in this book, state that Cherenkov radiation from FTL particles never will be observed. For such reasoning takes no account of the imaginary factor in the quantities involved.

Imaginary time, negative time

Until now, we have simply been recapping standard textbook physics. It is now that the speculation begins. Time, as we have seen, is an imaginary quantity, in the sense that it naturally involves the square root of −1; while in a similar sense, the three spatial ones are real. When a velocity greater than light is introduced, this condition changes. The time element becomes real and the spatial component, in the direction of motion, becomes imaginary, as the Lorentz factor is imaginary for velocities greater than that of light, i.e.

$$\gamma = \left(1 - \frac{v^2}{c^2}\right)^{-\frac{1}{2}}$$
$$= -i\left(\frac{v^2}{c^2} - 1\right)^{-\frac{1}{2}}$$

I would now like to propose the following substitution,

$$u = \frac{c^2}{v}$$

where u is obviously a sub-light velocity (as v > c). The physical justification for this substitution must wait until later. For now I ask for it to be accepted simply in order to explore its consequences.

Substituting the above two equations into the Lorentz transformation gives

$$x = x$$
$$y = y$$
$$z = ic \left(t' - \frac{z'u}{c^2} \right) \gamma'$$
$$ict = (z' - u\,t') \, \gamma'$$

where

$$\gamma' = \left(1 - \frac{u^2}{c^2} \right)^{-\frac{1}{2}}$$

Obviously, this set of equations is very similar to those of the Lorentz transformation for sub-light velocities, which was the original reason for sugesting the substitution. There are two differences: the first is the interchange of the coordinate $(z' - ut') \gamma'$, which is real and has the form of a spatial displacement in the direction of motion with an associated Lorentz contraction of γ'; and the coordinate $i\,c\,(t' - z'u/c^2)\gamma'$, which is imaginary and of a form usually associated with time. During the derivation of the proper time, we saw how useful i was in determining the physical nature of the quantity associated with it. This indicates that the term containing it in the above equations is associated with the quantity that now represents time. The similarity with the sub-light Lorentz term that represents time supports this. Similarly, the fourth term now looks exactly like the real spatial term we associate with the direction of motion. This is borne out in later chapters; for now we will just accept this interpretation.

The second difference between these super-light equations and the sub-light ones lies in the change of sign of the new time element. If we accept the identification of this as time, we are left with the conclusion that an observer who is travelling faster than the speed of light relative to us is also travelling backwards in time. Equivalently, we are travelling backwards in time relative to him, from the intrinsic symmetry implied by travelling backwards in time. This symmetry further implies that, just as on our side of the light barrier sub-light velocities add to produce sub-light velocities, so too must pseudo sub-light velocities sum to pseudo sub-light velocities, for observers on the other side of the barrier.

This pseudo sub-light velocity can be substituted into the Lorentz transformation of all super-light four-vector quantities, with similar results. For example, the mass-energy also becomes negative, as does sub-atomic spin and a host of other properties. All these can be explained by a reversal of time relative to observers on this side of the light barrier.

One criticism that springs naturally to mind, especially after the denunciation of FTL Cherenkov radiation, is: why do we not observe such reverse time particles? To answer this consider two objects, one on either side of the light barrier. We will start with them stationary, and pseudo-stationary, relative to each other. Now can we expect them to be attracted towards one another by the action of gravity, or do objects on opposite sides of the light barrier have a gravitational repulsion? Let's assume it is an attraction. We would therefore see the particles approach one another, but what would an observer on the other side of the barrier see? As his time runs backwards, he would see the objects move apart. Yet to him it is our time that is running backwards, and so he would reason that objects on different sides of the light/time barrier have a mutual repulsion. Similarly, if we begin by assuming that such objects repel we will find that they attract for the observer on the other side of the barrier. This contradicts the necessarily symmetric relationship between two such observers. But there is a way out of this dilemma if the particles do not interact via gravity.

We can reason the same way for all forces and, indeed, all interactions in general. Therefore there can be no interaction of any kind between objects on opposite sides of the light barrier. If such objects do exist, we have no way of observing them directly. There could be an entire universe moving backwards in time and we would never know! There might be, nevertheless, conditions – for instance when we get close to the light barrier – when some communication may be possible, and there may even be evidence in other branches of physics that something is going on on the other side of the barrier. In particular, the negative mass-energy associated with objects on the far side of the barrier is something we shall be returning to in later chapters, though from an entirely different angle.

In conclusion, we do have the possibility of travelling FTL, and as a natural consequence the possibility of travel backwards in time. We even have the possibility of crossing the time/light barrier with a finite amount of energy in a finite proper time – even if it does take forever as far as the rest of the universe is concerned.

Once we are on the other side of the light barrier, travelling backwards in time, what do we do then? Well, we could always cross back again. If we time it right we could return at whatever point in history we wish. As we have seen, we can get anywhere within the universe in a little under two years' travelling below the speed of light. By travelling super-light, or more correctly on the other side of the time/light barrier, we can arrange to arrive back here at any time. With a little planning, we could arrange to return to Earth after the passage of the same Earth time as our proper shipboard time. This is true FTL, and with it comes the power of travel in both space and time. With it also comes the possibility of undershooting our departure time, arriving back before we left and even interfering with our own departure. Once more we are back with the paradox with which Chapter 1 opened. It seems that this is still the only serious objection to time travel. Again, I will defer tackling this until later.

· VI ·

General Relativity: A Matter of Some Gravity

The universe is bent.

Albert Einstein, slightly misquoted

Space is curved! That was the conclusion of the second of Einstein's great revelations, general relativity. In this chapter will be considered the meaning, the evidence for and, most importantly, the results of this conclusion. The essential difference between Einstein's two relativities is that special relativity applies to flat, Euclidean space-time while general relativity applies to curved space-time. When this curvature is small, special relativity is an excellent approximation, just as Newton's relativity is an excellent approximation at low velocities. It is only in the presence of severe curvature, over large distances or long times, that the effects of general relativity manifest themselves.

Until now we have considered the effects of special relativity only in connection with observers moving at constant velocity relative to one another, largely ignoring acceleration other than as a means of attaining these velocities. Special relativity is quite capable of accommodating the relativistic effects of accelerated observers. The cumulative relativistic effects of acceleration are simply the sum, or more correctly the integral, of those associated with all the intervening velocities. (Again, for the full formal mathematical development interested readers should consult any of the numerous textbooks on special relativity.) In the universe in which we live, every object, every particle, even the individual photons that comprise electromagnetic waves exert forces upon each other. And all these forces produce acceleration.

There are four distinct forces in nature, the strong and weak nuclear forces that govern nuclei, and the electromagnetic and gravitational forces that we experience on our scale of existence. Surprisingly perhaps, gravity is by far the weakest of these. For example, the gravitational force of attraction between the electron and proton in the common hydrogen atom is 4.4×10^{-40} times weaker than the electromagnetic attraction.

Now both nuclear forces act over only short distance, of the order of the size of the nucleus. Although they have the essential role of holding nuclei together, beyond the nucleus they have no significant effect.

The electromagnetic force acts only upon charged particles, causing oppositely charged ones to attract and similarly charged ones to repel. Consequently, charged particles tend to distribute themselves in such a way that they cancel each other's influence, accumulating in approximately equal numbers of positively and negatively charged in every object from the hydrogen atom (one positively charged proton and one negatively charged electron) to the largest star. Where imbalances do occur, the electromagnetic force acts to redress the balance. For example, when clouds develop a net charge the result is lightning, in which electrons arc through the air to re-establish the balance within the cloud.

Conversely, gravity is always cumulative. The gravitational field from the electron in a hydrogen atom adds to that of the proton, and the field from every atom adds to that of every other atom in an object. And this is true of every fundamental particle that we know of or have even hypothesized. Consequently, if you pile on enough mass, gravity comes to dominance over all the other forces. With sufficient mass, gravity determines the motions of you, me and of the planets, the evolution of the stars and even the destiny of the universe itself. So wherever we are in the universe we experience the force of gravity, and along with it the inevitable acceleration.

The principle of equivalence

There is one very important law of nature which we now need, and I shall approach it from the viewpoint of everyday experience. If you step off a chair you do not fall at a constant speed to the ground. Instead you are accelerated towards the ground by the mutual attraction of you and the Earth. If the ground was not there you would fall to the centre of the Earth, but of course if the ground was not there there would be no Earth to accelerate you. Stand up and you can feel the Earth pulling down upon your body with the force of gravity. This force is the source of the pressure of the floor against your feet and the downward drag on every part of your body. When you begin to ascend in a lift you feel an increase in these sensations. Similarly, when you begin to descend these sensations decrease. Were you in a spacecraft in free space (a region of space sufficiently far from any large mass for the gravitational forces to be negligible), accelerating at 9.81 metres per second per second, you would experience exactly the same sensations as you do standing on the Earth. Essentially, you would find it extremely difficult to tell if you were in a closed room on an accelerating spacecraft, or in a stationary one on the Earth's surface. Gravitational and accelerated frames of reference, are virtually indistinguishable; they are, in fact, equivalent.

In practice, there are methods to distinguish between gravitational and accelerated frames of reference. One involves accurately measuring, as they fall, the separation of two balls dropped from the same height. In the accelerating spacecraft the balls would move along perfectly parallel courses, while on the Earth they would fall towards the planet's centre. Consequently, in the latter case the final separation of the balls would be less than their initial separation, though only very slightly (see Fig. 6.1). This is termed the tidal effect, as it is the cause of the tides here on Earth. A tidal force is the difference in the gravitational field between one point and another. This difference is the reason for the oceans here on Earth heaping up directly below the moon, and on the far side of the Earth from it. This gives rise to the twice-daily tides from which this force derives its name.

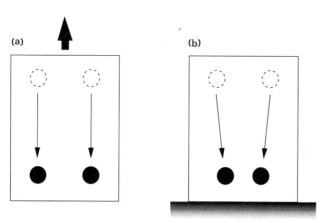

Fig. 6.1 The motion of objects: (a) in an accelerating lift in free space, and (b) in a lift in a gravitational field.

Apart from this tidal difference, the laws of physics for an inertially accelerated observer are in all ways exactly the same as for a gravitationally accelerated one. This is termed the principle of equivalence, and it assists us greatly in deriving the effects of gravitation. As a very simple, though none the less useful, example of this equivalence we can use acceleration to remove the effects of gravity. Suppose we drop a lift containing an observer from a great height – approximately infinite, say – towards a body such as the Earth. The acceleration of the lift exactly counteracts the gravitational force, and the observer experiences no forces within the lift except for the tiny tidal ones which we will ignore. Now the instantaneous velocity, v, of the falling observer, when he is at a distance r from the centre of the Earth, is given by:

$$v = \left[\frac{2\,G\,M}{r} \right]^{\frac{1}{2}}$$

where G is the universal constant of gravitation and M is the mass of the attracting body – the Earth in this example.

Life in a gravitational field

In Chapter 2, we saw that observers in relative motion experience time dilation. So if you were in the lift, and I were at a fixed distance r from the centre of the Earth, we can expect the rates at which time passes to be different for each of us. The exact amount of this difference we can obtain immediately from special relativity theory, by substituting into the time dilation equation the instantaneous velocity of the lift as it passes me. This gives:

$$\Delta t' = \Delta t \left[1 - \frac{(2\,G\,M)}{(r\,c^2)} \right]^{\frac{1}{2}}$$

where $\Delta t'$ is the time experienced by me, the fixed observer, and Δt that of you, the falling one. Note that it is the observer fixed in the Earth's gravitational field for whom time runs slowly, for it is he who is experiencing gravity. For the falling observer the effects of the force of gravity are balanced exactly by his acceleration; for him it is as if he were still in a region of space that was free of gravity.

We conclude, then, that observers in a gravitational field experience time dilation in just the same way as observers in constant relative motion. Time runs more slowly here on Earth than it does in the heavens, though the actual time dilation factor for the Earth is only 1·0000000008. On the surface of Jupiter, where the force of gravity is greater, this factor is higher and time runs more slowly. Similarly, at the surface of the sun time runs more slowly still. There are even places where time runs infinitely slowly, as we shall see in Chapter 7.

Similarly length, in the direction of the acceleration (that is, towards the centre of the attracting body), is contracted by this same gravitational Lorentz factor:

$$\gamma = \left[1 - \frac{(2\ G\ M)}{(r\ c^2)} \right]^{\frac{1}{2}}$$

Not surprisingly, the mass of an object in a gravitational field is similarly increased. Generally, all the relativistic effects associated with motion are exhibited by objects subject to the force of gravity. This is the basis of general relativity.

Gravitational curvature

Let's look now at one of the consequences of length contraction due to gravitation. From our knowledge of special relativity, it is obvious that this contraction is experienced only in the direction of motion of the falling observer – that is, towards the centre of the gravitational mass, in the radial direction. In the two directions perpendicular to this, lengths are unaffected, just as those perpendicular to the direction of motion are unchanged in special relativity. Consequently, if we measure the radius and the circumference of a spherical gravitational body their ratio is no longer 2π. Rulers placed in the direction of the radius will be shortened by the gravitational Lorentz factor. Therefore, the radius will be greater than for a flat, Euclidean space, as we can effectively fit more centimetres into the radius. Conversely, the circumference is unaffected. Therefore, the ratio of the circumference to the radius is less than 2π. For the Earth, as we have seen, the difference would be minute, as its gravitational field is small; but the more massive the body the greater the effect and the greater this difference from 2π. Similarly, the surface area of the Earth, and indeed any object, will also be less than $4\pi r^2$.

This result for the circumference and surface area should be familiar: it is identical to the situation discussed in Chapter 4 in connection with our friendly flatlanders. And, just as one of those two-dimensional folk should be able to reason that his universe is positively curved in a third dimension (provided he was possessed of the mental stature of Albert Einstein), our own Albert Einstein reasoned that our universe is positively curved in the neighbourhood of matter – positively, since the surface area of a sphere is less than it would be in a flat, Euclidean space.

This idea of curvature is a somewhat difficult one, for we are so used to thinking in flat, Euclidean terms. We know the Earth's surface is curved, yet we have difficulty fully appreciating what this means. In our everyday experiences we treat it as if it were flat; even the majority of our maps are flat. For example, Southern California is west south-west from Great Britain and you might therefore expect to head west south-west to fly from London to San Francisco; if you do, remind me never to get on a plane that you are piloting! The shortest route is north by north-west, over Scotland and the Arctic Circle – a course that traces out a great arc, the shortest distance between two points on a sphere. If you look at a globe this is obvious, but we are all far more familiar with flat maps and compass navigation. All this works extremely well over short distances, where the effects of curvature are very small, because of this, and because of the added complexity of dealing with curvature, we insist on thinking in essentially flat terms. Yet this does not prevent us dealing with both a curved world, and a curved universe, when we must.

The presence of mass, then, really does produce curvature. From the reduction in the ratio of surface area of a sphere to its radius we can conclude that in the neighbourhood of mass, space is positively curved. The effect of gravity, and consequently the curvature, decreases with distance from the Earth. Consequently, the curvature of space-time by the Earth is not closed as is the surface of a sphere. Instead, the effect of mass is to produce a dent in the surrounding space-time. As usual, the best way of depicting this is to drop one dimension and create what is called the 'rubber sheet' model of the distortion of space-time by gravity (see Fig. 6.2). The greater the mass the deeper the indentation, or gravitational well, that is formed. Additionally, these curvatures are cumulative, in the same way that gravity is. As we shall see in Chapter 7, given enough mass, space-time can be made to fold back on itself to form a closed surface, in the simplest case a hypersphere.

So what we three-dimensional equivalents of flatlanders call gravity is actually curvature in four dimensions. We really do live in a curved

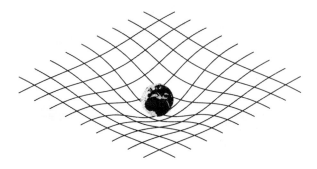

Fig. 6.2 Rubber sheet model: the presence of mass distorts the flat, Euclidean space–time continuum.

four-space. Gravity is simply the way in which we volume-landers observe this four-space curvature. It was this realisation that confirmed Einstein as the genius he undoubtedly was.

The evidence for general relativity

The importance of any theory lies in its ability to describe the physical universe. So let's look at the evidence for general relativity, starting with the verification of time dilation in a gravitational field. Though the effect is extremely small here on Earth, it is cumulative with time, and the accuracy of caesium clocks is such that we now have the necessary sensitivity to corroborate, or refute, the theory. The experiment involves using two such clocks that are synchronized at the outset. The first is placed in a laboratory here on Earth, subject to the time-dilating effects of the gravitational field. The second is placed in a 'flat' region of space – that is, one free of the effects of gravity. It is not necessary to remove the clock to an infinite, or even extremely great, distance to accomplish this; we must simply place it in a state of prolonged free fall. As we have seen, dropping it would be one way of doing this. But apart from being destructive, it would not provide us with sufficient time for measurable differences to accumulate, unless we were to mount a major space programme. Fortunately, there is a state of free fall that is sustainable almost indefinitely and that is fairly readily attainable: placing a clock in orbit. In such a state, the 'force' of gravity and that of acceleration are in perfect balance; just as they are for a falling object. We have all seen film sequences showing the absence of gravity on board orbiting spacecraft. The absence of gravity is the same as free fall, the same as being in free space, the same as being in a region of flat, Euclidean space: all are just different ways of saying the same thing. So placing one of our synchronized clocks in orbit will cause it to become increasingly advanced relative to the one that remains on Earth. Not at all surprisingly, the results of this experiment are in precise agreement with those predicted by general relativity.

A second experimental verification of general relativity involves the bending of light in a gravitational field. As photons have a mass-energy they will be deflected by gravity; this is predicted by both Newton's and Einstein's theories of gravity. General relativity, though, predicts twice the bending of that predicted by classical Newtonian theory. To test which is correct, we require a large mass with a fixed light source behind it. Then, as the source moves behind the mass relative to us, the time at which it disappears from view will be delayed due to the bending of the light from it (see Fig. 6.3).

The reason we need a large mass is that these effects are small, and the obvious one to use is the largest object in our neighbourhood, the sun. For a fixed light source we can use a distant star, the effect of whose motion is even smaller than the relativistic ones we are trying to measure. Usually, the intense brightness of the sun blots out our view of stars as they come into alignment with its surface. During eclipses, however, the sun's light is eliminated. From measurements made during total eclipses, the bending of light has indeed been shown to be in agreement with that predicted by general relativity – as, by now, you should expect.

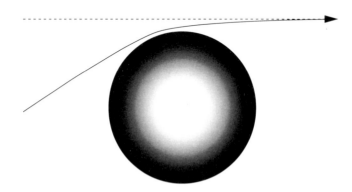

Fig. 6.3 The bending of light by gravity.

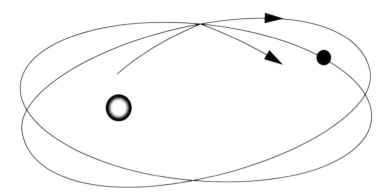

Fig. 6.4 The advance of the perihelion.

The final experimental verification of general relativity which I shall mention here is the advance of the perihelion of the planets. This was the first stumbling block for Newton's theories of gravity, and one that gave scientists a great deal of trouble for several centuries. The perihelion is the point of a planet's closest approach to the sun. On each orbit of the planet, this point advances slightly (see Fig. 6.4). Mercury, as the nearest planet to the sun, has the shortest orbit: 88 days. In addition, its orbit has the second greatest eccentricity (deviation from circular). The most eccentric orbit is that of Pluto, but as its orbit takes 248 years we have not yet had the opportunity to witness the advance of its perihelion. Mercury then, provides us with our best opportunity to observe this advance. Much to the embarrassment of Newton and his successors, the actual advance is one and a half times that predicted by his theory. It was one of the triumphs of general relativity that it finally accounted for the total perihelion advance.

The single cause of both the additional advance in the perihelion and the bending of light is the distortion of space and time in the presence of mass. (I do not propose to go into the mathematics here; as usual, interested readers can refer to any standard text for a full treatment of these phenomena.)

The bent universe

The universe is full of mass-energy – from high-density regions, such as the interior of stars, to the emptiness of intergalactic space, pervaded, as it is, with cool background radiation. We can therefore expect space to be positively curved by this mass-energy. Just as locally the actual degree of curvature depends on the local distribution of matter, so too is the curvature of the universe at large determined by the average density of matter. The mean curvature, as will be seen in Chapter 7, is of primary importance in determining the ultimate fate of the universe. Unfortunately, such is the scale of the universe that, to date, we have been unable to make sufficiently accurate measurements to determine its overall curvature.

There is nothing in general relativity that forbids the existence of space-time geometries with negative curvature; indeed, many such cosmologies have been hypothesized. (Again, any interested reader can find descriptions of these in the literature.) For our universe to have a negative curvature, general relativity requires the existence of a force of repulsion that dominates at great distances. There is no evidence for the existence of such a force, and for this reason I will make no further reference in this book to these negatively curved cosmologies.

So we can now add to our description of the universe of Chapter 1. Not only do we now know where and when we are – in terms of the proper time, of course – but we also know that the universe is positively curved due to the presence of mass. Whether there is sufficient mass to close this curve is a matter of some conjecture, and it is a question that we shall be examining in detail in Chapter 7.

· VII ·

Black and White Singularities: The Hole Story

What goes up, must come down?

The author

Jump up in the air and, after reaching a certain height, you fall back down. Jump harder and you go higher. Throw a ball into the air and it rises higher still. These examples demonstrate that, the faster an object is launched upwards, the greater the altitude it achieves before gravity drags it back down. Now, the further an object is from the centre of the Earth, the smaller the force of gravity acting upon it. Is it possible, then, to launch something so fast that it never falls back? The answer, surprisingly perhaps, is yes. What goes up does not necessarily have to come back down. Consider what happens when a torch, or better still a laser, is pointed upwards. When does the light – which is travelling at a finite, if extremely fast, speed and, as we have seen, is affected by gravity – fall back? Obviously never. At least not on the Earth. So if at some speeds objects can escape and at other speeds objects fall back, then there must be a critical velocity at which objects just fail to come back – at which they just succeed at escaping. Not surprisingly, this is called the escape velocity.

For the surface of the Earth this escape velocity is approximately 11.2 kilometres per second, give or take a little depending upon where we are on its surface. It is less at the top of a mountain than it is at sea level. It is also less at the equator than at the poles; the Earth's rotation produces a small but measurable counter to the gravitational field there, in addition to the convenient bulge in the Earth's surface caused by this rotation. It is no coincidence that the major launch sites for spacecraft are positioned as close to the equator as the respective governments can arrange. Not that spacecraft are launched at the escape velocity: quite apart from the fact that doing so would instantly smash every piece of delicate equipment on board and kill the crew, there is the problem of getting the craft up to speed. All these problems are solved by using a continuous reaction drive that steadily, though still with considerable force, accelerates the craft. None the less, the same considerations that make the escape velocity very slightly less at the equator represent a considerable saving in the required energy – fuel – and hence the cost of launching a spacecraft. Fortunately, we do not need to consider the practical aspects of launching objects into space and can concentrate on ideal examples.

In general, the escape velocity for a planet, or any other object, is given by

$$V_c = \left(\frac{2\ G\ M}{r}\right)^{\frac{1}{2}}$$

where G is the universal constant of gravitation, M is the mass of the planet and r is the distance from the centre of the planet to the point at which escape is desired.

This expression is the same as that of the curvature of space in the presence of mass. It is no coincidence, but simply a consequence of the fact that the velocity at which an object is thrown upwards is the same at which it returns – in other words, the escape velocity is simply equal and opposite to the velocity that an object will reach when dropped from infinity to that height. We shall make use of this reciprocal relationship, between the escape velocity and the velocity attained in falling from infinity, later.

The escape velocity does not depend on the mass of the object – it is the same for a feather, a human being or a spacecraft. Of course, the effort required to get an object to the escape velocity does depend on its mass, which is why the payload of a spacecraft is so critical.

The escape velocity also depends on the starting point, the distance r from the centre of the object to that of the planet. The greater the height, the less initial upward velocity is needed to escape from the gravitational well. Conversely, the lower down this well we start, the harder it is to get out. If the distance between the centres of the objects was zero, it would take infinite velocity to escape. In practice – here on the Earth, for example – the surfaces intervene, preventing any such coincidence of two centres. What then of matter at the centre of a planet? Well, once inside the planet the gravitational pull of all the

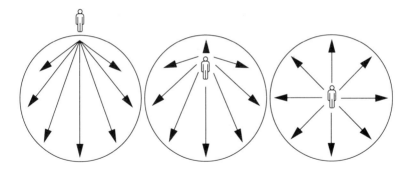

Fig. 7.1 Gravity on the inside of bodies.

matter above acts upwards. The deeper we go the more matter there is above us, until, at the heart of a planet, the total matter in every direction is the same (see Fig. 7.1). At this point there is literally zero gravity. Consequently, Edgar Rice Burroughs' Pelucidor would be a far different place from that which he described in his books.

Let's return now to what happens above the surface. The equation also tells us that the greater the mass of a planet the greater the upward velocity needed to escape. It is easier to escape from the surface of the moon (mass about $\frac{1}{80}$ that of the Earth) than from the surface of the Earth; with the resistance of the atmosphere, that makes it more difficult still here on Earth. Yet the escape velocity from the surface of the moon is still some 2.4 kilometres per second, for the moon has only a quarter the radius of the Earth – and objects have to escape from a point that much nearer the centre.

On more massive worlds we can usually expect the escape velocity to be correspondingly greater. On Jupiter, the largest of our local family of planets, it is 60 kilometres per second. To escape from the 'surface' of the sun, which is 1000 times more massive than Jupiter, requires a velocity of 620 kilometres per second. And the sun is by no means the largest object in the universe. Usually, the more massive these bodies are the larger they will be, and this corresponding increase in radius will offset to some degree the increase in mass; although, if we keep the mean density of the body constant while piling on more matter, the mass will grow faster than the radius, and consequently the escape velocity will continue to increase. Generally, with more massive objects gravity tends to pack the atoms more closely together, increasing the density and hence raising the escape velocity still further.

So what keeps everything in the universe – every planet, every tree, you and me – from imploding under the action of gravity? Well, everything is made up of atoms (plus a few other rare particles that only form under the extremes of high-energy physics, which we can ignore). Atoms are made up of electrons, protons and neutrons. Electrons are tiny, 10^{-28} gm, negatively charged particles that are commonly found orbiting the much more massive, positively charged, atomic nuclei. In turn, these nuclei consist of collections of positively charged protons and electrically neutral neutrons, in approximately equal numbers. As for the neutrons, they are essentially the combination of a proton and an electron, and are so stable – unlikely to break up into their two components – that they warrant a name of their own. Now the electromagnetic force which holds the electrons in orbit about the oppositely charged nuclei also prevents similarly charged nuclei coming too close together. This repulsion is opposed by the gravitational attraction, of course, but for an isolated pair of hydrogen atoms this electromagnetic repulsion is 10^{36} times greater than the gravitational attraction. Consequently, atoms tend to stay apart. The nuclei themselves are held together by the strong and weak nuclear forces, but these act over extremely short range, and for most purposes can be ignored outside the nucleus. Between atoms the electromagnetic force is generally neutralized by the presence of the negatively charged electrons. It is only when we attempt to force nuclei closer together than the electron orbits that the repulsion comes into play. Matter exists then in a balance between these forces.

Gravity, though, is always cumulative. The more mass, the greater the force. So what happens when greater and greater amounts of matter are brought together, under, for example, the action of gravity? Well, initially the temperature goes up. All that mass falling together liberates considerable energy in the form of motion. On the atomic level it manifests itself as heat. This heat serves to keep matter apart, at least until the object has had time to cool by radiation. Pile on enough mass and we have a planet – after it has cooled down sufficiently. Pile on more and the heat generated is enough to start nuclear fusion: hydrogen nuclei fuse to form helium, helium to form beryllium and carbon, and so on up the periodic table to produce the heavier elements. This we call a star. Given enough time, even a star begins to run out of energy. It then cools down and gravity restarts the process of collapse. Although this whole business is complicated by the occasional explosive loss of mass, of which novas and supernovas are the most spectacular examples, the general trend is one of collapse.

Let us suppose, then, that more mass is piled on, and that no significant amount is lost in explosions or radiated in the normal business of shining, which is generally the case. Then we can expect the escape velocity from the body's surface to increase, even if its mean density was to remain constant. For a star the density will increase, which will further increase the escape velocity. Eventually such a star will become what is called a white dwarf, whose density is so great that a single teaspoonful would weigh several tons. The existence of white dwarfs is no mere flight of fancy. From observations of the motion of binary stars – two stars sufficiently close to orbit each other, and which exist in abundance throughout our galaxy – it is possible to determine the mass of each. Now, provided that they are near enough for us to get their radii by direct measurement, it is a simple matter to calculate the mean density of each. We are very fortunate in that our second nearest neighbouring system, Sirius, is just such a binary pair and the smaller of the two, Sirius B, is indeed a white dwarf.

Neutron stars

If the piling on and consequent compression of matter in a star continues, eventually the atoms will be squashed so close together that there will be no room left in which the electrons can orbit. Strong though the electromagnetic force keeping matter apart is, eventually it must lose to the cumulative effect of gravity. At this point the electrons in all the atoms are forced into the protons of neighbouring nuclei, in the process forming neutrons. We then have a neutron star – a star composed entirely of neutronium, with a density of some 10^{14} times that of water, a pinhead of which would weigh millions of tons. Such densities are, of course, unknown on the Earth, or for that matter anywhere else in the local neighbourhood of our solar system. Although the Russian scientist Lev Landau predicted the existence of neutron stars in 1932, within a year of the discovery of the neutron, it was not until 1967 that the observations of radio astronomers in Cambridge confirmed their existence. Yet it was several more years before it was realized that what they had found were indeed neutron stars.

What these astronomers actually had were observations of very rapid, and remarkably regular, pulses of radio signals (at up to 30 pulses per second), from sources that were invisible. Not knowing what it was that was producing these pulses, their discoverers named the source pulsars. They are still known by this name today, and many textbooks dating back to the late 1960s and early 1970s refer to the mystery of these radio signals' origin.

The reasoning behind the eventual identification of these rapid, regular pulses with neutron stars is quite simple. Every celestial body we know of rotates: the Earth in 24 hours, the sun in approximately 25 days. Now this rotation involves a large amount of rotational energy, and when a star collapses that energy must be conserved. Just as an ice skater rotates faster as she draws in her arms, so too does a star speed up as it contracts, although, in the case of a star the size of the sun (radius 700,000 kilometres) shrinking to the size of a neutron star (radius 12 kilometres), the speeding up would be considerable, even allowing for the loss of a great deal of energy by radiation. To date, neutron stars that rotate as swiftly as once every $\frac{1}{30}$th of a second, down to ones that rotate as 'slowly' as once in $4\frac{1}{3}$ seconds, have been found. Celestial bodies also commonly possess a magnetic field, and this too will become 'concentrated' as a body collapses. In the case of neutron stars this intense magnetic field, rotating along with the star, carries with it electrons. It is the periodic sweeping of these clouds of electrons around the star that is responsible for the radio pulses we receive.

The period of these pulses is simply the rate at which the neutron star rotates. Now we can expect this sweeping electron beam, and other frictional interactions, to slow down the neutron star, and this is exactly what is found. With time, every rotating star is indeed slowing down. We can also expect the speed of rotation to be directly related to the age of the neutron phase of a star's life cycle, and this too is the case. One of the earliest theories of the formation of neutron stars, that of Baade and Zwicky, is that they result from the collapse of supernovae. The remnant of just such a supernova, which was recorded by Chinese astronomers some nine hundred years ago, is the Crab Nebula. And at its heart there is indeed a pulsar, a neutron star, the youngest yet found and, as we expect, the one with the fastest rate of rotation.

Occasionally neutron stars speed up, suddenly rotating faster and giving rise to pulses with a greater frequency. The most reasonable explanation – for we cannot observe these tiny objects directly – is that from time to time neutron stars undergo a little more collapse. A fraction of a millimetre is enough to account for the observed increases.

So what happens to the escape velocity as a neutron star collapses still further, and what if even more mass gets in on the act? In both cases it will increase still further. So just how far have we come as regards escape velocity? Well, for our neighbourhood white dwarf, Sirius B, it is some 5000 kilometres per second, which is fairly high by Earth standards. For a neutron star, of mass 1.4 times that of the sun, it is some 170,000 kilometres per second – which is higher still, over half the speed of light. Now if such a neutron star should contract to one quarter of its diameter, or if we pile on sufficient additional mass, we would reach a point at which the escape velocity from the surface reaches the velocity of light. At this point no material object, no electromagnetic wave, nothing, can ever escape from the body's surface. Consequently, it can no longer even be seen. This is a black hole.

Black holes

The theory of black holes, bodies from which even light itself cannot escape, has been around for a surprisingly long time, though they only became fashionable in the 1970s, when the discovery of their close relative, the neutron star, lent credence to the possibility of their existence. Most of the recent theoretical work was done in the early twentieth century by Schwartzchild, building on Einstein's general relativity. The implications of these, and subsequent results, we shall look at in a moment; first, a little history.

The story of the black hole actually goes back much further, predating both general and special relativity. In fact, we do not need general relativity to derive the theoretical existence of black holes; Newton's gravitational theory gives the same answer for the conditions under which a black hole forms. All that is necessary is to substitute the speed of light, c, into the equation given at the beginning of this chapter for the escape velocity. With a little rearranging we then have:

$$ r = \frac{2\,G\,M}{c^2} $$

So when an object of mass M collapses to a radius equal to or less than r it will become a black hole. We call this the Schwartzchild radius or the event horizon, because it is a surface up to which we can observe events, but beyond which we cannot.

This is a fairly simple result to derive from Newton's laws of mechanics, and one that was first derived in exactly this way by the mathematician Laplace in 1799. The result remained a little-known intellectual curiosity for almost two hundred years, until we were able to develop a technology capable of providing at least tentative confirmation. I say 'tentative' because we cannot observe black holes directly, even if one happened to be conveniently close – which unfortunately is not the case. Or perhaps I should say fortunately, as their gravitational field makes them the most voracious objects in the universe.

Even though we cannot observe black holes directly, the distortion they produce in space-time, their gravitational field, remains; so we can observe their effect on any nearby matter and, in particular, on nearby stars. This leads us to our first candidate for the title of black hole. Some six thousand light years away in the constellation of Cygnus, the giant star HDE 226868, weighing in at twenty times the mass of our own sun, has a tiny, invisible, binary companion. This companion, at five times the mass of the sun, has a diameter of only a few kilometres. The gravitational attraction between this pair causes them to circle one another in a mere six days. Yet could the companion not be just another neutron star? No, because it is simply too heavy. A neutron star has a fixed density, and there is a certain critical mass, or equivalent size, at which it must become a black hole. Substituting a mean density for mass in the above equation for the Schwartzchild radius (assuming the body is spherical) gives:

$$r = \sqrt{\frac{3c^2}{8\pi\,G\,\rho}}$$

This tells us exactly how big an object of a particular density can be before it must become a black hole. It also shows that matter – given enough of it, however rarefied – will eventually fall within this radius and become a black hole.

Let us look at the implications of this. An object formed of something as dense as neutronium (density 10^{14} gms/cc) will form a black hole when its radius is greater than 4×10^4m. But this equation tells us that, if an object is only as dense as water (1 gm/cc), given enough of it (a sphere of radius greater than 4×10^{11} m) it too must form a black hole. This is also true of the atmosphere that you are breathing at this moment; if it extended far enough, it too would fall within its Schwartzchild radius. This holds even for the scattered matter – the planets, stars and interstellar dust – that comprises the universe as a whole, for there is no need for the matter to be uniformly distributed so long as it extends far enough. This is a very important point, for the universe itself may well lie within its Schwartzchild radius.

Does this mean that the universe is a black hole? As we shall see shortly, it cannot be, for it does not have the correct properties – but this does not mean that it will not eventually become one. The problem of determining whether the ultimate fate of the universe is to become a black hole reduces to that of determining whether there is enough mass to halt the expansion. For then, at some time in the far future, the universe will collapse. Conversely, if there is insufficient mass then the universe will continue expanding forever, spreading out and getting ever thinner and cooling as it goes.

To answer the fundamental question of the long-term prospects of the universe, we have to determine its size and density. The size is relatively easy to determine. Given the known age of the universe (for which time it has been expanding at the speed of light), and neglecting for the moment any considerations of curvature (which we can correct for later), we get a radius of 15,000 million light years. Unfortunately, from astronomical measurements of the stars and interstellar material, the estimates of the universe's average density are tantalizingly ambiguous. Approximately one-tenth of the required mass to produce an eventual collapse has been found. But this is only an estimate, and fails to take into account the mass of stars hidden within the vast and abundant stellar clouds; dark stars and galaxies, objects that emit radiation only at frequencies that we cannot yet detect; undetected neutron stars; invisible black holes; and perhaps even black galaxies. Add all these in and the answer may well be that the universe is closed in time – that some day it will stop expanding and collapse back to its original infinitely dense point. Unfortunately, by definition we cannot measure this invisible mass. As our technology advances we are forever improving our observational abilities, and continually finding more mass, yet we are still far from definitively resolving the question of the ultimate fate of the universe. However, as we shall see in Chapter 8, by examining the way in which the universe began we can gain some insight into its ultimate fate.

Infinite curvature

We saw in Chapter 6 that the force we call gravity is a geometric distortion of space-time, that in the neighbourhood of matter, space-time gets 'stretched'. So what happens near a black hole? Going back to the model of the rubber sheet in which one spatial dimension is suppressed, we have a circle from which nothing can emerge. This circle represents the surface, the event horizon, of the black hole. Since the gravity becomes immense as we approach this circle, this implies a great degree of geometric distortion. Consequently, the gravitational hole is deep; in fact, infinitely so (see Fig. 7.2). At the event horizon the flat, horizontal sheet of space-time is curved to the point at which it becomes vertical. It is, quite literally, a hole in space-time.

What happens, then, to an object that is dropped into a black hole? Obviously, it will be accelerated by the gravity. This acceleration will continue at an ever-increasing rate until the object reaches the event horizon. At this point, at what speed will the object be travelling? As we saw earlier in this chapter, the speed at which an object falls from infinity is at all points the same as that of the escape velocity. Therefore, any object dropped from infinity must be travelling at the speed of light when it reaches the event horizon of a black hole.

Maybe dropping something from infinity worries you, for the object would take an infinite time to fall. As an alternative, imagine throwing the object towards the Earth from a certain height, at the escape velocity corresponding to that height. The object would still reach the surface of the Earth at the escape velocity from the surface. So, instead of dropping an object from infinity we can throw it downwards from any other height with a correspondingly higher initial speed. As it falls, the acceleration will increase the velocity. The initial velocity need not be excessive, because the escape velocity falls off rapidly with distance.

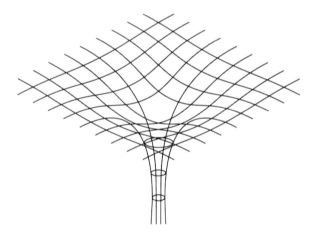

Fig. 7.2 Black holes produce an infinitely deep distortion in flat, Euclidean space–time.

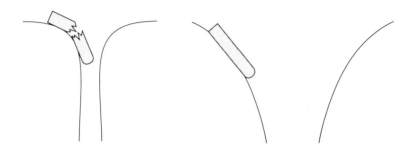

Fig. 7.3 Tidal curvature: objects which would be torn apart entering a small black hole would survive the fall into a larger one.

It also depends only on the mass of the attracting body and not on its radius. So, if, for example, the sun were to shrink sufficiently to become a black hole of radius 3 kilometres, the escape velocity at the distance of the Earth's orbit would remain 42 kilometres a second. It is a simple matter, then, to cause an object to fall at a speed equal to, or greater than, the escape velocity.

So when we drop something from infinity into a black hole it must attain the speed of light when it reaches the event horizon. Once within the black hole, the acceleration continues, provided the surface of the black hole is below its Schwartzchild radius; which is always the situation, as we shall see shortly. Again we have found a way of reaching, and exceeding, the velocity of light, at least in theory. This is just the gravitational equivalent of our inertial examples of Chapter 5.

In Chapter 6 we saw that there is one difference between gravitation and acceleration – the presence of tidal forces. Not surprisingly, the tidal forces near a black hole can be quite severe. In the near neighbourhood of a small black hole the tidal difference in gravity, over even quite small distances such as the length of the human body, can be tremendous. In fact, near the event horizon of the black holes that we have discussed so far the tidal forces are so great that anything the size of a human being would be literally torn apart. Ironically, the bigger the black hole the smaller the tidal forces.

In terms of the geometry of black holes, those 'space-lines' (coordinate lines of our rubber sheet model) that intersect such holes change from horizontal to vertical. With a small black hole this change must be accomplished in a short distance, while for a more massive hole it is achieved over a larger one. Consequently, as the stick in Fig. 7.3

plunged into the small black hole it would be torn apart by tidal forces associated with the sharp curvature of space-time; but the same stick would survive a fall into the larger hole. The important factor is the ratio of the object's size to the size of the black hole. For a human being to survive the tidal forces of a black hole, it would have to have a mass approximately equal to that of our galaxy. But there is no reason to suppose that black holes of this size, and much greater, do not exist.

Even so, the neighbourhood of a black hole is a very dangerous region, and not one to be entered lightly. Apart from the tidal disruption there is all the other matter that the gravity of the voracious black hole will attract. This will be both falling in, and orbiting at terrific speeds. Additionally, a lot of charged material will be dragged around by the rotating residual electric and magnetic fields of the black hole, which are similar to those in the neighbourhood of a neutron star, but rotating faster still due to the black hole's smaller radius. Indeed, the amount of raw energy liberated in the neighbourhood of a black hole is expected to generate a blue nimbus immediately above the event horizon. This surrounding aura of intense blue light is the result of the orbiting matter, trapped within the gravitational well of the black hole, colliding at high speed. In turn the fragments of these collisions add to the orbiting population. Energy is released by these collisions in the form of radiation, and with the loss of this energy the fragments take up tighter orbits. With more objects orbiting in a smaller volume of space the chances of collision increase, and the smaller the radius of the orbit, the faster the objects move and the more energetic these collisions will be.

Typically then, the history of matter in the neighbourhood of a black hole is one of fragmentation while spiralling down towards the event horizon. Associated with this is a release of radiation of increasing energy. So as we look ever deeper into the gravitational well of a black hole we observe radiation of increasing intensity progressing: from infra-red heat in the upper reaches; through the visible spectrum towards the blue lower down; to the high-energy ultra-violets and beyond as the event horizon is reached. To an outside observer these energies are lowered by the red shift of the radiation as it struggles up out of the well. There is no such amelioration for any black-hole voyager. The last visible shell of a black hole is therefore intensely blue. Consequently the event horizon is often referred to, rather poetically, as the 'blue event horizon'.

A trip to a black hole

Let's take another of our imaginary journeys, this time into the heart of a black hole. For the purposes of this exercise we shall assume that you are an observer in a craft falling towards a black hole, while I shall remain in orbit at a comfortably safe distance. From my point of view, as you fall, light from you has to crawl up the sides of the gravitational well. It crawls at the speed of light, of course, but it has ever greater distances to cover. On the way out it gets stretched, becoming more red shifted the deeper in the well you are. An alternative way of looking at this is that the increasing speed of recession from me will produce a progressive red shift, so I would see you becoming fainter and fainter, as light from you shifted more into the red. In theory, you would never disappear completely from view; in practice, the red shift would quickly become so great that the light, and all other electromagnetic radiation from you, would grow far too weak for any detector.

Suppose you were to send a signal to me every second as you are accelerated away from me. Each successive signal has to travel further up the sides of the infinite well, and so takes longer to reach me. To me, you would appear to move more and more slowly the closer you got to the event horizon. Indeed, it would take you forever to get there, at least as far as I am concerned. After an infinite time, as you reached the event horizon you would appear to be frozen in time. So for me, watching you fall into a black hole is the same as watching you accelerate away from me up to the speed of light. Again, this is just the gravitational equivalent of the inertial examples of Chapters 3 and 5.

But what would you experience? Well, you would see all that stuff that was falling in with you – all of which would be lost to me, and to any other outside observers, in the extreme gravitational red shift. Because of your increasing speed, length contraction would exactly balance the gravitational stretching of space, and so for you the well would be of finite depth. Similarly, time dilation would ensure that the total proper time of your fall would also be finite. Naturally, we will have chosen a sufficiently massive black hole so that you will arrive intact at the event horizon. Your speed then will be equal to that of light!

To recap, from my viewpoint the hole is infinitely deep and you appear to take an infinite amount of time to reach the 'bottom', the event horizon. In an infinite time, with an infinite fall, there is no problem with reaching the speed of light. To me, and to the rest of the universe that remains outside the black hole, it simply never happens. From your point of view, the entire fall is completed in a finite proper time. Relative to your starting point, though, you really have attained the speed of light in a finite time. This should be familiar! Again it is just the gravitational equivalent of our earlier inertial examples. So you have arrived at the blue event horizon travelling at the speed of light. What happens next? We come, at last, to the interior of a black hole.

Unfortunately, Newton's theories give us no clues to what you might expect to find within a black hole; for this we must turn to the work of Schwartzchild and his successors. Necessarily we have to rely on theory. Even if we had a convenient black hole to examine, we cannot, by definition, see beyond the event horizon – unless, that is, we ventured within, and then there would be no way of informing anyone outside about what we find.

Beyond the blue event horizon

Inside the black hole the mathematics gets really interesting. To start with time becomes space-like and space becomes time-like. By 'space-like' is meant all those properties we normally associate with space, for example the ability to move both forwards and backwards. Similarly, 'time-like' describes all those properties we associate with time, such as being unable to move backwards, or to communicate with objects that are moving in the other direction. Now there are three space-like dimensions but only one time-like one out here in the universe. Inside a black hole there are also three space-like dimensions and one time-like one. So which one of the space-like ones does the changing? Not surprisingly, it is the one in the direction of motion, the one in which your velocity exceeds c – the radial direction. The two directions, perpendicular to this, are unaffected. Naturally, it is the time dimension that becomes space-like.

This should sound familiar – it was exactly what we saw in Chapter 4 when we introduced velocities greater than the speed of light into the equations of special relativity. In both cases we are dealing with the far side of the light barrier. In passing the event horizon you attained, and exceeded, the speed of light. This is yet another example of the equivalence of inertia and gravity; though in the case of gravity, the space is no longer Euclidean. The curvature of space-time does not affect the arguments in any way beyond introducing tidal effects, which we have reduced to negligible proportions for your safety.

In Chapter 4, no mention was made of the terms 'space-like' and 'time-like'; this was intentional. There was no need, or rather the substitution of the factor c^2/v (where v was a velocity greater than that of light) removed this necessity. Without this substitution, some confusion of properties attributable to the various dimensions would be understandable.

What significance, then, should be attributed to the terms 'space-like' and 'time-like' dimensions? Well, if something lives in water, dies in the air and has scales I would call it a fish, even if the first time I saw it it was flying through the air. Similarly, a winged creature which flies, but which under certain circumstances is observed to dive and swim underwater, I would insist on calling a bird. What I would not do is call the first one a fish-like bird, or the second a bird-like fish. So if a dimension has all the properties of time – is time-like – I would hazard that it is time in reality. And if a dimension has all the properties of space – is space-like – I would stick my neck out and call it space. From here onwards I shall drop the 'like' nomenclature, as I don't!

Where does this leave you, our intrepid black hole voyager? Inside the black hole, of course, but with the radius of the black hole now the dimension of time, and with the other three dimensions forming a hyperspherical surface about it. At least, this is the simplest symmetric case. If this is a little too much to picture – which quite frankly it is for me – we can always suppress one, or even two, of the three spatial dimensions without losing any of the usefulness of the model, since two of them are unaffected by your motion (see Fig. 7.4).

Within the black hole, the radial direction possesses all those properties we associate with time. In particular, all events progress in the same direction. If you harboured any hope of getting out of the black hole, forget it – you cannot even turn around, at least not without crossing this space's light barrier. For a black hole is a complete universe unto itself.

As a further consequence of the acceptance of the radius as time, all the matter within it is moving backwards in time relative to matter outside. This is only to be expected, since on entering the black hole you crossed the light barrier. As we saw earlier, this itself implies that no communication across the time/light barrier is possible. But this is just the definition of a black hole, though now it has been arrived at from a different standpoint.

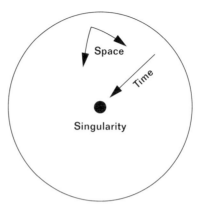

Fig. 7.4 The space–time geometry of a black hole.

In your black-hole universe, all the matter occupies the surface volume of the black hole. This matter is moving in through time (which is now) along the radial direction towards the centre of the hypersphere. Consequently, all matter is collapsing in towards this central point, and it is an intrinsic property of black holes that this collapse must continue. Even electromagnetic radiation is constrained to move inwards. These are well-known results from general relativity, but now we see that they are as much a consequence of the temporal nature of the radial dimension as they are the effect of gravitational forces.

Both interpretations predict that all the matter, mass and energy within the black hole will fall into the single point that is the centre. And it really is a point – not small, but of absolutely zero size. At this point all objects will be crushed to infinite density. Worse still, all the matter will arrive at the centre at exactly the same moment, only to be crushed into a single infinitely dense point of zero radius. Such a point we call a singularity.

This is a singularity in space-time, not just in space – in other words, it is a single moment in time and point in space. That the point is a singularity in space-time is implicit in the four-dimensional nature of general relativity theory. This is an extremely important point, in every sense, as we shall see later.

So for you, our weary space traveller who has survived the infinite fall into the galactic black hole, there is an even stranger fate in store than being torn apart by tidal forces at the event horizon. You will be

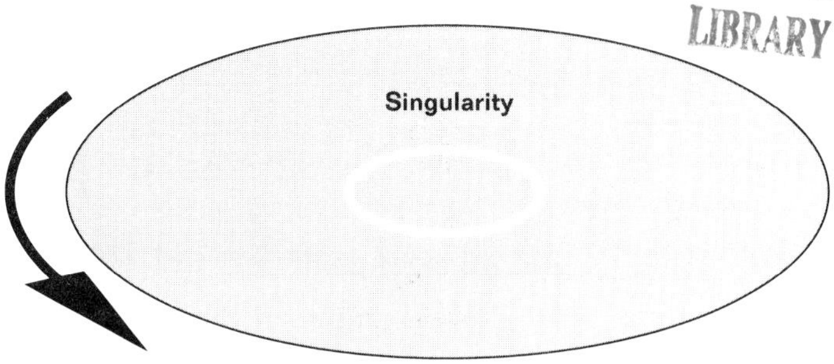

Fig. 7.5 A rotating black hole, with one spatial dimension omitted. The rotating causes the event horizon to bulge at the equator into a circularly symmetric ellipse. The singularity is similarly drawn into an infinitely thin circle directly beneath the equator.

crushed to a point, simultaneously along with every other object that has fallen into the black hole. This was why I elected to remain safely outside!

Yet there is some hope for you. In the neutron phase of a collapsing star on its way to becoming a black hole its rotation was conserved; indeed, our whole evidence for the existence of neutron stars is the regular pulses that these rotations produce. It is extremely likely that black holes, even galaxy-sized ones, will also possess a rotation, for galaxies usually possess a considerable rotation of their own. The mathematics of rotating black holes is not as simple as that of static ones, as the system is no longer spherically symmetric. We shall therefore not go into any detailed analysis here, but will restrict ourselves to the relevant results. In particular, for a rotating black hole the singularity is not a single point, but an infinitely thin circular ring in the hole's plane of rotation (see Fig. 7.5). Most importantly for you, an object falling through this ring will not be crushed to a point, but will continue on through unharmed. Of course, any object or part of an object coming into contact with the ring will suffer the same fate as it would in a non-rotating black hole. So, provided the ring is of sufficient radius to permit you, our black hole voyager, to pass cleanly through, you would survive.

Quantum nature
There is even hope that you could survive the fall through a non-rotating black hole. Both the special and general relativity are classical

theories; neither takes account of the quantum nature of matter. Classical theories of matter – those which deal with it on the macroscopic scale – treat matter as if it were made of discrete billiard balls. In particular, they hold that matter at the microscopic level comes in two fundamentally different types: solid isolated particles, and ethereal extended electromagnetic waves. This approach works to a degree, but at the beginning of the twentieth century certain anomalous results started appearing that suggested that the so-called fundamental particles such as electrons and protons sometimes exhibited wave-like properties. Also, it was found that electromagnetic waves sometimes behaved like particles. The truth, at least as far as our present level of understanding has established it, is that all objects have some form of intermediate nature. Particles are believed to be something like a packet of concentrated waves (see Fig. 7.6). Similarly, electromagnetic radiation can exist in single wavelets (see Fig. 7.7). The mass-energy equivalence of special relativity is a consequence of this.

This duality in the nature of mass-energy introduces both a discreteness (or quantum nature) and a certain degree of uncertainty to all of physics. Einstein strongly contested this idea of uncertainty in nature; his objections were summed up by his famous phrase 'God does not play dice with the universe.' Which goes to prove that no one is right all of the time. More about the discrete, quantum theory of nature later; for now it is sufficient to know that this theory exists. At fundamental levels and at very high energies, such as particles near the speed of light or matter in extremely high densities, this quantum discreteness becomes important. Classical laws, even those of relativity, do not take quantum effects into account, and a full unified theory of quantum relativity does not yet exist; so a definitive theoretical prediction of what occurs at a quantum singularity is not known. In practice this is unlikely to be of assistance to you on your voyage to the centre of the black hole, though it is worth noting as a possible limitation of the general relativistic model.

Before going on to see what happens beyond the centre of a black hole, I would like to recapitulate some of the significant facts about the interior. First, in agreement with the conclusions of Chapter 5 regarding the shape of space-time in the vicinity of matter, a symmetric black hole is a hypersphere with time as the radius. Second, it is an entirely different space-time continuum, and one that is moving backwards in time relative to this one, until it 'ends' at its singularity. Just because the black hole's universe ends at this point does not stop us continuing

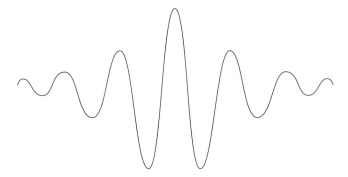

Fig. 7.6 The wave nature of particles.

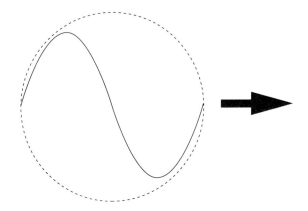

Fig. 7.7 The particulate nature of waves.

our imaginary voyage. For we still have to discover the ultimate fate of you, our explorer, whom we wisely dropped into a rotating black hole of galactic mass.

Beyond the singularity: the white hole

All the matter that has fallen into the black hole arrives at the central singularity, or within the ring of a rotating black hole, at the same moment. Indeed, by its very nature the singularity exists only at this moment in time. This is not a stable position for so much mass-energy, and the whole must continue on through and out into yet another universe. From the point of view of this third universe, all the mass will appear at the same moment where it will subsequently expand.

Almost certainly, this occurrence will be explosively violent.

For now we shall put aside concerns about your safety and consider the simple case of a symmetric black hole with a single point singularity. We can expect all matter, as we know it, to have been converted to pure energy by the incredible temperatures generated by its coming together at the singularity. Subsequently, as this energy expands into the new universe, it will cool and then recondense into isolated lumps of matter – electrons, protons and neutrons. When it expands and cools still further, these particles will unite to form atoms. If there is enough mass, this process will continue to form stars, planets and galaxies.

In passing through the singularity there is no exchange of space and time associated with crossing the event horizon, or equivalently light barrier. Consequently the time axis remains as it was, except that the arrow of time now points outwards along the radius. In other words, events must now proceed in such a way that the radial time component will always increase. This is a white hole, a four-dimensional hypersphere, expanding outwards along the radial dimension of time (see Fig. 7.8). It is the antithesis of the black hole.

There is no reason to suppose that this alternative universe had any mass-energy of its own before the advent of the white hole. It may have had, but we simply do not know. Essentially, if there were no mass and correspondingly no space-time continuum, the white hole would be quite capable of creating it. It is possible, then, that the new universe is one of the white hole's own making.

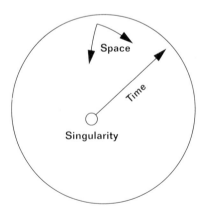

Fig. 7.8 Expanding, hyperspherical, balloon universe.

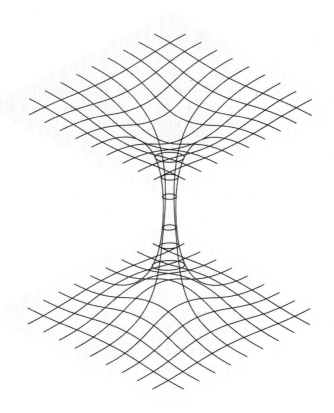

Fig. 7.9 A wormhole linking two separate space–time continuums. As usual, one dimension has been suppressed, and in reality the circles are the surface of spheres.

As for the singularity, this will have vanished. For it exists only as a point in four-space-time – that is, at a single point in three-space, and at a single moment in time, the initial one of the white hole's creation. Immediately afterwards the singularity will no longer exist anywhere in the new space, for its moment has passed; though it does exist in the past. If it were to persist for any amount of time it would form a line in space-time. We are able to observe a white hole – that is, the effects of the singularity – but we cannot observe the singularity itself. It is simply too short-lived; a singularity is ultimately ephemeral.

So what has happened to you, our hole explorer? Well, we dropped you into a rotating black hole where the tidal forces, which continue into the centre, are countered by the rotation. The conservation of angular momentum ensures that the white hole will also be rotating about the same singular ring, allowing you to emerge – unscathed, we hope – in this third universe, along with everything else that had ever fallen into the black hole. Your time again proceeds in the direction it did before you entered the black hole, although now you are two universes removed from both me and your starting point. Not only has your home universe long since run its course, all its history having passed during your fall into the black hole, but the black hole itself has vanished. As for the ring singularity through which you emerged, this too has vanished, at least as regards the three-space you now inhabit. For you, then, there is no way back. Passing through another black hole, will, instead of returning you to this universe, take you on into further new realms.

The above description of black and white holes is the conventional one, and does not explicitly rely on the possibility of travel backwards in time. This black and white hole pair is often referred to as a tunnel, or wormhole, in space-time (see Fig. 7.9) The black-white wormhole links two space-time continuums, two universes – the old and the new. But before we go on to explore this new universe I would like to look again at the beginning of our own universe, this time in a little more detail.

· VIII ·

Cosmology:
In the Beginning

Nothing can be created from nothing.

Titus Lucretius Carus

Once upon a time there occurred a very singular event. It was an event to end all events, or rather to begin them all, for this was the beginning of the universe. It happened at a particular place and at a particular time, which is what makes it singular. As for before that moment... well, there was no 'before', because time itself began at that moment. To talk, therefore, of some form of creation is a contradiction in terms, there being no time for the act of creation to have taken place in – and, incidentally, no matter from which the universe could have been constructed. There remains the question of where, in the broadest possible sense of the word, the matter came from. To answer this we must necessarily look elsewhere than in the non-existent past.

First, let's look more closely at the early history of the universe to see if its evolution can give us any clues to its ultimate origins. As we saw earlier, there is considerable evidence that the universe is expanding, and has been for all time. It follows that at the beginning everything was concentrated into an infinitely small, infinitely dense point. From here everything could only get bigger and less dense, as the universe expanded and cooled.

Four-dimensional balloon
As an analogy imagine a four-dimensional balloon, a hypersphere, with the three-dimensional curved surface of space expanding in time. Now a four-dimensional balloon is perhaps a little difficult to envisage. If we drop, as usual, one spatial dimension, we are left with a simple three-dimensional balloon without loss of generality. The curved surface represents space and the radius time. As this balloon expands,

objects embedded in space move through time in what we will arbitrarily call the positive direction.

Such a model has several features to commend it other than just its simplicity: space is unbounded yet finite; time has a particular beginning; space expands; and the curvature is positive, a property we ascribe to the real universe by dint of the matter within it. On the large scale, matter is fairly evenly distributed in the universe, which creates a large-scale uniform curvature; again, in agreement with the simple model. Matter's habit of aggregating causes local variation in the curvature, and consequently the rate at which time passes. This can be accommodated in the model by introducing local dents into the balloon's surface. The general features of the model, then, are similar to those of our universe. And so we are back with our familiar balloon model; I said we would be returning to it. Now, though, we have sufficient evidence to adopt this as a working model for the real universe – though we are at liberty to discard it if it conflicts with our observations.

So the real universe appears to be a hypersphere with space, the curved three-dimensional surface, expanding outwards along the positive radial, time. Does this description remind you of anything? It should – it is identical to that of a white hole, which we discussed in Chapter 7. The positive, radial nature of the time and the explosion of matter from a point singularity are so strongly suggestive of a white hole that identification is obvious. This, then, offers an answer to the question of the origin of the matter in our universe. It was formerly moving backwards in time within an alternative universe inside a giant black hole. This in turn was the remnant of yet a third universe, one which in a sense anteceded our own in a universal cycle of birth and death – a cycle in time, in the most literal sense.

It is, of course, pointless searching for the singularity that was the origin of our universe, just as it is pointless seeking the centre of the universe, which in the only meaningful sense is the same thing. It is pointless looking for the singularity in space, anyway, for there isn't one – at least, as far as the surface of our hyper-balloon universe is concerned. This singularity has long since vanished, at the very moment when the universe began. If a singularity were to exist for any length of time it would trace out a line in space-time; it would then be a three-space singularity and not a four-space one.

Let's look at some of the consequences of identifying our universe as a white hole. Perhaps the most important arises from the fact that the universe arose from the black hole remnant of a previous universe, a veritable cosmic phoenix. That this previous universe was within its Schwartzchild radius strongly suggests that our own is also within its Schwartzchild radius, and will ultimately collapse to give birth to yet another universe and so on. Conventional Big Bang theory leads to the same conclusion: that the universe is within its Schwartzchild radius and must some day become a giant black hole.

To see this, consider again the moment of the universe's formation. At this moment it had infinite density. It can be argued that this is only an approximation arising from the classical nature of general relativity, and that quantum effects may reduce this description to a mere 'extremely dense'. But this does not affect the following argument in the least. The important point is that, for some time after the beginning, the density was such that the universe must have been within its Schwartzchild radius. As all matter within the universe moves at, or below, the speed of light, by definition it cannot have escaped beyond this radius. Consequently, all matter within the universe must still be within its Schwartzchild radius. This follows directly from the fact that the universe started at a particular point at a particular time. This argument is based only upon the accepted view of the universe's origin and not directly upon the possibility of backwards time travel.

Actually, at least one current theory hypothesizes a short period at the beginning of the universe when conditions were such that the speed of light limit did not apply. The theory postulates that during the first few moments the universe underwent a rapid inflation, with space expanding at a rate much greater than c. To invalidate the above argument – that the universe is within its Schwartzchild radius – it is necessary to assume further that this inflation carried sufficient matter beyond this radius to open the universe. If we accept this second assumption we must reject the above account of the origin of our universe's mass-energy, for there is no reason to suppose the existence of a previous universe within its Schwartzchild radius. So for now we will reject this second assumption and reserve judgement on the general inflation model, as it does not affect the previous arguments.

We are left with the conclusion that the universe is indeed a hyperspherical white hole, with the arrow of time pointing outwards in the direction of the increasing four-dimensional temporal radius. Because it is within its Schwartzchild radius it will eventually revert to a black hole, with the arrow of time pointing inwards towards its hyperspherical centre. As a result, all the matter currently in the universe will be available for the next cycle. Similarly, our present universe must contain all the matter that was present in the last one.

At what point does general relativity predict that a white hole will revert to its black state? On this point it is a little complicated. A white hole remains white for half eternity, after which it will form a black hole and collapse for the remainder of eternity. But eternity is forever, and so what is half eternity? And what tips the balance? Again, as yet we do not have the conceptual tools to answer this – though later we will.

What, then, of smaller stellar- and galactic-sized black holes? As we saw earlier, in a flat, Euclidean space these produce infinitely deep, par-allel-sided wells. In our curved, hyperspherical space-time we can expect this curvature to warp the sides of these gravitational wells, causing them to converge to a common point in space-time: the origin of the universe (see Fig. 8.1). As the universe ages, these holes grow in size and number until, literally at the end of time, they coalesce to form a giant black hole. This will then take all matter back through time to a simultaneous rendezvous at the singularity origin of the next cycle.

So our universe is probably a white hole, the black hole remnant of a previous one. At some time in the far future it will again become a black hole, the source for yet another universal cycle. But is it really another cycle? If the matter in a black hole is going back in time, then will it not simply go back to the start of this universe, forming a closed loop in time, a cycle of birth and death that repeats in an endless monotonous cycle of birth and death that repeats.... ?

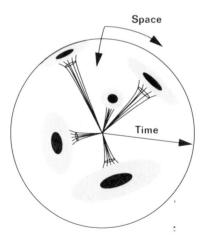

Fig. 8.1 'Bottomless' black holes in a closed space–time.

A hideous thought – one which might have appealed to the billiard-ball physicists of the nineteenth century, but one that ignores the indeterminacies that underlie modern quantum theory. In an indeterminate quantum universe there can be no guarantee that the particles will exactly trace out their former courses. A universal cycle of a single closed loop is not possible, and with each cycle a different universe must be created.

Let us for a moment return to the paradox with which this book opened. Suppose that in one universal cycle a man lives to have a son, but in another cycle is murdered by a mysterious stranger before he can become a father. Let us further suppose that the mysterious stranger is in fact the son who has voyaged through a black hole into this new universe. Now there is no longer a paradox. In this new universe he is quite at liberty to prevent this alternative father from fathering an alternative of himself. We have also answered the question regarding the ultimate fate of a black hole voyager with which Chapter 7 ended. The universe into which you would emerge would be similar to our present one, but with a few changes – maybe only in the existence of alternative patricides!

Unfortunately this does not remove all objections to time travel, for so far we have ignored the fact that two different universes exist at the same moment in time – in fact three, counting the one that is moving backwards in time (although, as we have seen, there can be no inter-action between this and the forward-moving ones, so it, at least, poses no problem). This does not hold for a universe moving in the same direction of time as ours. Worse, why just two universes, two universal cycles? Why not three, four or more? And if they exist, where are all these other universes? Have we, as it were, simply substituted one paradox for another? Not quite. This new 'paradox' arose from considerations of the origin of our universe and the identification of it with a white hole. The solution of the original paradox was simply a consequence of this. But the existence of alternative universes does pose a genuine problem, the resolution of which will finally lay our original paradox to rest.

Before answering this final question, I would like to look at some other branches of physics where evidence exists for the possibility of reverse time travel.

· IX ·

Entropy and
the Arrow of Time

The Moving Finger writes; and having writ,
Moves on: nor all thy Piety nor Wit
Shall lure it back to cancel half a Line,
Nor all thy Tears wash out a Word of it.

Edward FitzGerald (trans.),
The Rubáiyát of Omar Khayyám

We have already touched upon the idea of energy, and the basic concept is familiar to everyone. We all know what it is to be tired, to 'lack energy' – it is simply when we are unable to perform work. And this is precisely the technical definition of energy. Whether we are talking about lifting a spacecraft into orbit or just lifting yourself out of bed, it all requires energy. But mention 'entropy' and even science graduates groan. Which is rather ironic for, although the mathematics of entropy is more complicated than that of energy, it is just as important and perhaps even more fundamental a quantity. It is also just as familiar – so much so that it is usually completely taken for granted, and consequently goes unrecognized. Let's demonstrate this with the assistance of a few simple illustrations.

Imagine you are watching a game of snooker on television – or, for any American readers, pool. The balls hurtle around the table, bouncing off each other and the cushions. Now suppose all these balls come to rest together in a triangle. What would you suppose was going on? I'm pretty certain you would conclude that the film had been played backwards. I did the first time I saw this, and I was correct, as you would be. So how did you know that this was what had been done? After all, it is just possible that the balls could come to rest in this manner, though extremely unlikely.

Now for a home experiment. Almost fill a glass with tap water, gently add a spoonful of milk and leave it for ten minutes. Is the milk still together? It was when it was on the spoon, so why isn't it now? Stir the water. Does the milk separate out or get more mixed in? Just how would you go about separating it back out? Is it even possible? Well, yes, if you were to take enough trouble, enough time and, most importantly, enough energy – but compare that to the energy required to mix it. It is a general rule that it is always easier to destroy than to construct, to break down than to build up.

Life is sometimes quoted as an exception to this rule. It is not! To maintain the ordered structure of your body you break down food-stuffs to produce energy. These foodstuffs in turn were constructed through the release of energy, and so on. Each time we look at the whole environment of any system that involves ordered structuring, we find that there is a net energy loss. This is true even at the level of plants, for were it not for the slow heat death of our sun there would be no photosynthesis. It may well be that the purpose of life is simply to facilitate the heat death of the universe.

All things tend towards disorder – humans and other living crea-tures get older, the sun, the very universe itself runs down, using up irreplaceable fuel and cooling towards an eventual heat death (unless, that is, it should start to collapse back upon itself – but I am getting a little ahead here). The point of these somewhat depressing illustrations is that they are all examples of the same process. Yet so much taken for granted are its manifestations that we do not normally associate them with each other, or generally even notice them. This is why we are so unfamiliar with their collective name, entropy. The common property of all these examples can be summarized in the statement: the entropy of a system tends to increase with time. By 'time' here we mean with the direction, or arrow, of time pointing forwards. This is a weak state-ment, in the sense that it uses the words 'tends to'. Yet this is the best we can do, as we must allow for the possibility that things can evolve towards lower entropy – that, for example, snooker balls could return to their start positions, or that the milk could spontaneously separate out of solution.

Mathematically, the definition of entropy involves the probability of a system being in a certain state. In the light of the snooker table example above this should not surprise us too much, for, as already stated, it is possible that the balls could come together to form the V shape we normally associate with the start of the game. But that would be extremely improbable; the most probable state is one in which they are scattered over the table. Similarly for our spoonful of milk in a glass of water. The most likely state of the system, once it has been left to reach equilibrium, is one in which the particles of milk are scattered randomly amongst those of the water. This maximum probability state is also termed the maximum entropy state.

Entropy, then, is a measure of the disorder in a system. It reflects the most likely outcome of any series of events, and systems tend towards states that have greater entropy. In time, then, any system – a glass of milk and water, you, me and indeed the entire universe – will evolve towards a state of maximum entropy. But there are a couple of other examples that I would like to introduce before we consider something as complicated as the universe.

A simple entropy model

Consider a draught board with four draught pieces placed on one of the central squares. Label them arbitrarily A, B, C, D. Now take a dice and throw it. If it shows one, two, three or four spots when it lands move draught A up, right, down or left respectively. If it shows five or six leave the draught where it is. Continue this process for draughts B, C and D. Repeat this thirty or forty times and, if a piece comes to an edge and the dice 'decides' it should move off the board, take it off and place it back on at the opposite side of the board. Now where would you expect the pieces to be? Together where they started, together somewhere else, or scattered randomly about the board? If you picked anything other than the last either you are using loaded dice or you are the sort of person I like to bet against!

Let's look at the probabilities involved. After the first round there is a reasonable chance that they are still together on the central square (81 to 1 against), after two rounds (6561 to 1 against), and so on. Suppose the pieces have moved so many times that any bias involved due to their initial position has been eliminated. Now the odds that the pieces are still together on the square on which they started are 64,416,777,216 to 1 against. How did I calculate these odds? Well, the odds against one piece being on a particular square are just the number of squares on the board to one. For all four pieces it is just this number raised to the power four. In fact the odds that any particular configuration of the labelled pieces, any particular state, occurs are the same. This probability is what determines the maximum permissible entropy of the system – how disordered it can become.

To see this more clearly let's look at a simpler system still: a board with only one square. On such a board we know where the pieces are, there is only one possibility and so the disorder is least, and both the actual and maximum entropy are zero. On a board with two squares there are two possible locations for each of the four pieces, or 2^4 (16) possibilities for the whole system. These are:

```
[ A B C D ] [           ], [ A B C     ] [        D ],
[ A B   D ] [     C     ], [ A     C D] [   B      ],
[   B C D ] [ A         ], [ A B       ] [      C D ],
[ A   C   ] [   B   D ], [ A        D ] [   B C    ],
[   B C   ] [ A     D ], [   B   D ] [ A   C    ],
[     C D ] [ A B       ], [ A         ] [   B C D ],
[   B     ] [ A   C D ], [     C     ] [ A B   D ],
[       D ] [ A B C     ], [           ] [ A B C D ]
```

The maximum entropy of this system is 4 (see Appendix B). Increase the number of squares to 4, and we have 4^4 (256) possibilities (which I do not propose to list) and a maximum entropy of 8. This demonstrates a very important property of entropy – the greater the number of possibilities the greater the maximum entropy of the system. The actual entropy reflects the actual state of the system at a particular time. In a perfectly ordered state, which we shall define as all the particles on their initial square, the entropy is zero; but, as we have seen, this system tends to evolve towards a state of maximum disorder, of maximum entropy. At any moment in time the actual entropy will fall between zero and this maximum.

What has all this to do with entropy in the real universe? Let us look at major differences between this model and any real systems. In the real universe no two objects can occupy the same space; fundamental particles are indistinguishable – all electrons, for example, are the same; the boundary conditions – what happens at the limits of the containers – are different; the objects are not limited to specific points – we say the space is continuous, not discrete; and their movement is also continuous. We shall consider each of these objections in turn.

The first of these, that the objects cannot occupy the same volume, is not true for all types of matter. For example, if you shine two coloured lights so that they intersect, they will pass through one another. In fact, any number of photons can simultaneously occupy the same space. Conversely, two people, two snooker balls or even two electrons cannot. The model, then, holds well for light waves in a mirrored box, but not as well for a gas in a perfectly elastic-sided one.

It is a simple matter to modify our model so that it can also cope with this second type of matter. We apply an exclusion principle in that no two draughts may simultaneously occupy the same square. Now the simplest model is one comprising four squares, for which there are 24 (4!) possibilities. Draught A can occupy any of the four squares. Choose any one of these four and that leaves a choice of three for draught B; then two for C, and finally only one place is left for D, $4 \times 3 \times 2 \times 1$ or 4! (4 factorial). The maximum entropy of this system is less than 5; approximately half that for the four squares without this additional constraint. By imposing this restriction upon our particles we have limited the possibilities, and therefore reduced the maximum entropy.

The second difference between the draughts of our examples and the fundamental particles of nature is that fundamental particles do not have labels. We cannot write A, B, C and D on four electrons – what would you write with? We are at liberty to take the labels off the four draughts, and apply the second set of rules by which no two may occupy the same square. The simplest case, with four squares, has only one possibility – all squares occupied. Remember, it does not matter which draught is on which square: all are the same. The maximum entropy is zero. All this new rule has done is again to reduce the number of possibilities, and hence the maximum entropy, in any given situation. The simple model, then, is easily modified to reflect the nature of real matter, at least regarding occupancy of space.

Now let's look at the third difference between our model and the real universe: boundary conditions. Again, this is just a change in the rules, and does not significantly alter the conclusions for either type of particle – those that can and those that cannot simultaneously occupy the same position. Essentially, so long as the boundary conditions do not affect the number of possibilities they have no effect on the entropy of a system. It is also worth noting that a space that is curved back on itself has no boundaries, and in principle the situation is similar to that of the draughts model above.

I would like to tackle the last two differences, those of the discreteness of position and velocity, together; the reason will become apparent shortly. The model is intrinsically discrete, the draughts can only occupy whole squares and not lie half on one square and half on an adjacent one, while the universe is continuous. Or is it?

Quantum discreteness

As mentioned in Chapter 7, one of the major developments of the twentieth century was that of quantum physics. Now the word 'quantum' itself means the smallest value of a particular quantity that we can measure, which intrinsically implies a discreteness. This does not mean there is a smallest unit with which we can measure the position of a particle, nor does it mean there is a limit to the accuracy with which we can measure its velocity, but there is a limit to the accuracy with which we can measure both simultaneously.

Classical Newtonian physics stated that, in principle, provided you knew both the position and velocity of all the particles in a system you could predict its state, the position and velocity of every particle at any time in the future or past. Conversely, modern quantum physics states that this information is intrinsically unobtainable, for even one particle. This law, Heisenberg's uncertainty principle, quantizes the combined quantity – action – formed by the product of position and velocity. Quantum physics also states that action can only occur in discrete integer units of Planck's constant. The value of Planck's constant is very small, and consequently the discrete increments are so tiny that on the macroscopic scale, with which we are familiar, the universe appears continuous. But at a fundamental level, quantum theory simultaneously imposes a discreteness on the position and velocity of every particle in the universe.

Our real universe, then, is not too different from our model, except that it is very much larger. At least now it is, for at the time of its origin it occupied a single point; though what constitutes a single point in the quantum sense is another question altogether. It raises again the problem of resolving the classical nature of Einstein's relativities – so useful for dealing with the universe on the macroscopic scale, with its blatantly quantum nature on the microscopic one – and I do not propose to tackle that question here. The resolution of these two, possibly inconsistent, views is still being sought. Indeed, it is only in the last two decades that any headway at all has been made in this field; the most significant by perhaps the world's leading living theoretical physicist, Professor Stephen Hawking. Interested readers are recommended to obtain at least two degrees in mathematics before attempting to read any of his formal papers!

Quantum and relativistic physics, though, are not incompatible. Action, for example, is Lorentz invariance. All inertial observers will agree on both the fundamental unit of action and on the value of any measurement of action. The universe, then, is not only discrete, but every observer agrees on the amount of discreteness.

The discrete nature of the universe is difficult to appreciate, for on the human scale everything appears continuous. Our perceptions are simply too coarse to appreciate so fine a detail. For example, when we look at a television screen we see a continuous piece of moving action, yet what is actually being presented is a set of twenty-four discrete images every second. Human vision is such that we cannot detect anything that happens within so brief a timespan as one twenty-fourth of a second; consequently, rapid viewing of images causes them to run together in an apparently unbroken sequence.

Maximum entropy

Let's get back to comparing our model with the real universe. There are, of course, many more particles in the real universe than draughts in our model. Both this, and the larger size of the universe, merely make the actual number of possibilities, and consequently the maximum entropy, correspondingly greater in the real universe. Otherwise, the model holds quite well.

In principle, we could determine the maximum entropy of the universe. All we need is the size of the universe – which, as we have seen, we get immediately from its age and geometry; the maximum permissible velocity (c, the speed of light); the number and type of particles; and the total energy of the universe. This last quantity acts to limit further the maximum entropy by reducing the number of possibilities. For example, if one particle were travelling sufficiently fast it would possess all the available free energy in the universe, and consequently every other particle would have to be at rest. Once we have all this information, calculating the maximum entropy of the universe is simply a matter of: multiplying each of the three dimensions of the total volume of space by the range of velocities (0–c); dividing by the quanta of action; and determining all the possible arrangements of the matter in the system. Simply? Well, in principle, at least, it is no more difficult than for our draughts model – the numbers are just very much larger. As action is Lorentz invariant, measurements of entropy, as defined in this model, are absolute – the same for all inertial observers.

The importance of any model lies in what it reveals about the real universe. The draughtboard model above tells us that the actual entropy falls between zero and the maximum, and that this actual entropy will increase, with time, towards this maximum. The model also shows that the larger the board the greater the number of possible configurations (possible locations of the draughts). And as the number of possibilities increases, so too does the maximum entropy. Expanding the board, then, causes the maximum entropy to increase. Extending this to real three-dimensional systems, we can conclude that the maximum entropy of a system increases with increasing volume. This is a strong result in that the maximum entropy of a system always increases with increasing volume, compared to the actual entropy, which merely tends to increase.

The converse of the above statement is also true, and the maximum entropy of a system decreases with decreasing volume. This is obvious from the above arguments. The actual proportionality depends on the statistics of the particles, whether they obey the exclusion principle or not; but this is irrelevant to the present argument.

That the maximum entropy increases with volume implies that in an expanding universe, such as our own, the maximum entropy increases with time. Remember that this is different from the actual entropy, which falls between zero and the maximum, and also 'incidentally' increases with time. I use quote marks because, although there is no evidence in the above arguments for the correlation between actual and maximum entropy, it is perhaps more than just coincidence that both increase with time.

At the beginning of this chapter the idea of entropy was introduced with a series of examples. If you pause for a moment to reconsider these, in particular the snooker balls bouncing about the table, you will see that the definition of entropy and the direction, or arrow, of time are inextricably intertwined. This has caused much speculation as to the existence of some connection between time and entropy. We have seen in this chapter that there is a correlation between time and maximum entropy: the universe expands in time and maximum entropy increases with volume. This adds support to the idea that time and actual entropy are related. If we say the proven result is a strong principle, then this latter would be a weak one. This is the best we could hope for, as we must always allow for the possibility that the actual entropy will decrease.

Entropy in a contracting universe
We come now to another question that we hope our model will help answer. What happens to the actual entropy in a contracting universe?

We know that the actual entropy of any system must lie between zero and the maximum entropy, and also that the maximum entropy will be decreasing in a contracting one. So, if the maximum entropy is decreasing, there must come a point at which the actual and maximum entropies are equal. And if the system continues to shrink, the actual entropy must also decrease. So at some point in a contracting system – a collapsing universe, for instance – the actual entropy must begin to decrease.

Yet why should the actual entropy wait until the moment at which the maximum entropy equals it before decreasing? And how is it that all the particles within such a universe will conveniently distribute themselves randomly at precisely this moment in time? Now we are not just bringing in the boundaries of our system; we are shrinking the whole space uniformly. To illustrate this, consider again our draught-board model. Let us assume the board has eight squares on a side, and that there are just two draughts which lie two squares apart. For simplicity we shall adopt the rule that the draughts will not be allowed to occupy the same square, and we shall assume that the state of minimum entropy occurs with them both touching. We shall also assume that the closer together the two draughts are, the less the entropy. For our present purpose we need only assume that the system is not in a state of maximum entropy, as the probability that the system reaches minimum entropy in two moves is obviously greater the closer together the draughts are at the start.

Now we are ready to shrink our entire draughtboard space by a factor of two in both directions. The squares themselves cannot shrink, just as our quanta of space-velocity cannot alter, and we cannot just throw away the outside squares because there might have been particles on them. Besides, in a real closed space there are no outside ones to 'throw away'. Instead, we simply merge every two by two set of squares into one, so retaining the discreteness of our model (see Fig. 9.1). For simplicity, we will assume that the dice dictates that neither draught moves. Consequently the two draughts are now adjacent and the entropy is at a minimum, though the maximum entropy is not. There are still a number of possible system configurations; we have just arranged it so that the actual one in the above example is the one of least disorder.

The contraction of the real universe would also have to occur on a point to point basis, for the size of the quanta of space-time is fixed. We can therefore conclude that both the actual entropy and

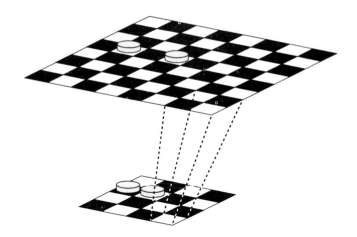

Fig. 9.1 A contracting system: each group of four squares contracts into one, the maximum entropy decreases and the actual entropy tends to decrease.

the maximum entropy of the contracting universe would decrease too. It could be argued that we artificially biased this model by supposing that the draughts did not move, but this just simplified the problem and, in principle, we could take this into account. Allowing for the possibility that the entropy could increase in our shrinking draught-board is equivalent to admitting that entropy can decrease in an expanding one – that is, that entropy could increase in a contracting universe, but that it is unlikely to do so. What we can say, from this example, is that the entropy is most likely to decrease in a contracting system. Generally, we can draw the weak conclusion that the entropy of a system tends to decrease with decreasing volume. This answers the question of what happens to the actual entropy in a contracting universe. It does not have wait until the maximum entropy is equal to it before beginning to decrease, any more than the actual entropy in an expanding universe must at all times equal the maximum entropy. Consequently, the particles within a contracting universe are no longer required to be conveniently distributed at a particular moment.

What consequences does this have for the way in which events proceed in a contracting universe – one in which the actual entropy is decreasing? If we look once more at the examples with which this chapter opened, but now with the entropy decreasing, the snooker balls would come together at their starting position; the milk would separate out of solution; people would become younger; and the universe would contract back towards a point. What, then, of the direction of time's arrow? As we saw in Chapter 7 in connection with black hole theory, in a contracting universe time runs backwards and the arrow of time points inwards, in the opposite direction to that of an expanding one. This agrees perfectly with all these, or any other, examples of decreasing entropy. To summarize, we have shown that the maximum and actual entropy obey the following strong and weak laws respectively: the maximum entropy of a system increases with increasing time and decreases with decreasing time; and the actual entropy of a system tends to increase with increasing time and tends to decrease with decreasing time.

These results should come as no surprise after those of previous chapters. Time, as we have seen, is just another geometric dimension. Contracting universes are associated with black holes, just as expanding ones are associated with white holes. The direction of time in both is inextricably linked to entropy, the physical manifestation of time's passage. This also provides a physical meaning for the arrow of time, which points in the direction in which time is changing and indicates whether it is increasing or decreasing. The arrow's direction, then, is inextricably interwoven with both entropy and geometry. This is yet another affirmation of the geometric nature of time, and of its similarity to the three spatial dimensions. As for the laws of entropy, these too are perfectly commensurate with the concept of reverse time.

A point of general interest concerns the entropy of a black hole. As we saw in Chapter 7, a black hole can still be observed by its gravitational well. From this we can determine its size and shape, and also its entropy; for the entropy of a black hole is simply proportional to its surface area.

I have saved until the end of this chapter one major objection to the linking of entropy with the arrow of time. There were two reasons. First, I wanted to develop the necessary background for understanding the problem, and second, I needed to provide readers with sufficient information to resolve the problems it raises. So if you wish to resolve the following dilemma yourself, pause before reading its solution.

Poincaré's dilemma
Suppose we have a finite number of atoms in an isolated, perfectly elastic box – i.e. one from which no energy can either enter or escape.

As we have seen, this is not a trivial example, for the universe is a similarly closed system in which the total energy in conserved. Now, for our closed box there are only a finite number of states – combinations of position and velocity – in which the atoms can be. Given enough time, every possible configuration of the particles within the box must occur. Afterwards, some arrangement must recur. Of course, some configurations are more likely than others. A roughly even distribution (high entropy) is far more likely than one in which all the atoms are clustered in the bottom left-hand corner (low entropy). This actually makes the repetition of a particular configuration more likely. Consequently, the entropy of the system will have returned to a former value.

If all configurations have occurred, then at some point the maximum entropy must have been reached. Subsequently, the system must change to one of lower entropy. This is allowed for in the classic law of entropy by the phrase 'tends to increase'. Yet, over a sufficiently long period, this maximum entropy configuration must repeat time and again. Consequently, the system oscillates between states of high and low entropy. For roughly half the time the entropy will be increasing and for the other half it will be decreasing. Accepting this as a model of the universe would imply that it is just coincidence that currently entropy is increasing, and that at some future time it will start decreasing. So can we expect that at some point in the future we will begin getting younger, as the sun draws back its energy? All the evidence so far tells us no. So Poincaré's model tells us that this should happen, while experience assures us it will not. This is Poincaré's dilemma and it has caused a questioning of the classic law of entropy that every experience affirms.

The resolution of this, like so many other problems of cosmology, is that the real universe is expanding. Poincaré's model is a static one in that the box remains the same size. Consequently the number of possible states of the system, the maximum entropy, is fixed. It is analogous to the model of the static universe that gave rise to Olbers' paradox. It is no coincidence that night and day became equally bright in Olbers' static universe as the energy distributed itself evenly throughout space; rather, this is just the maximum entropy state. Poincaré's model, then, only holds for a static universe, which, as we have seen, is unstable and must contract. And in such a contracting universe entropy would decrease.

The real universe is analogous to an expanding box in which the number of possible states is increasing. Therefore the probability of a pattern repeating becomes less with time, as in our example of the expanding draughtboard. In our expanding universe, then, the actual entropy is free to continue to increase. It increases towards a maximum with time, but this maximum itself is increasing; and, I would hazard, probably at a greater rate than the actual.

X

Bottomless Seas, Limitless Wells

This truth within thy mind rehearse,
That in a boundless universe
Is boundless better, boundless worse.

Alfred, Lord Tennyson

Remember when you were first taught that people had once believed the world was flat? Maybe you laughed at their ignorance. The feeling of superiority is a very satisfying one, and, provided it does not become a habit, perfectly normal. What you did not remember on that occasion, and probably do not now, is the time you were first told that the world was round. It was so long ago and you were undoubtedly very young. Yet there must have been such a time, for it is most unlikely that you would have arrived at this conclusion by yourself. Left to your own devices, it is not the sort of thing that you realize. That is just how it was for our ancestors.

Disconcerting as it may seem, there is no direct evidence to suggest that the overall human intelligence quota (IQ) is still rising. Some cynics might say that there is all the evidence in the world to suggest that it is not. It really depends on whether there is any evolutionary pressure working in favour of intelligence. Even conceding for the moment that there is, the rise from one generation to the next is imperceptible, and it takes many generations for the average intelligence to show any measurable increase. In such a long-lived species as ourselves this process requires considerable time. We can safely assume, then, that our ancestors were just as intelligent as we are, at least for the past few thousand years.

How, then, do we account for their amazing level of ignorance? Quite simply, we are more knowledgeable. Knowledge and intelligence are quite different things. Intelligence is an inherent quality with which we are born, while knowledge is what we pick up along the way – the total sum of our experiences. And these include not only our direct experiences, but also the indirect ones that other people share with us through the means of speech, the written word, pictures and so on. In general, we gain experience through what is called time binding, the general process by which experiences are stored for later generations. This our ancestors lacked – at least to anything approaching the same degree that we possess it now. They simply did not have maps and satellite pictures to show them that the world is round. Their direct experience taught them the exact opposite – that the world was flat. Look around you. Do your immediate surroundings suggest a round world or a flat one? If you are honest, you will admit that our ancestors had something. We are just too small in comparison with the size of the Earth to appreciate its curvature directly.

One thing our ancestors did have were ancestors of their own, the immediate ones of which could pass on their knowledge. Unfortunately, from their own experience, these ancestors could only teach their young that the world was flat. How much more difficult it was then to contradict not only the evidence of their senses, but also the experience and authority of their elders.

Round or flat, there are several questions that eventually come to mind. If it is round, why don't the Australians fall off? Of course, we know of the existence of gravity, but our ancestors did not. Still, a flat Earth possesses its own problems. How big is it, where does it end, and what is beyond it? Naturally, our ancestors posed these questions themselves, and, just like us with our gravity, came up with explanations; explanations which, admittedly, would not hold up before the rigorous scientific methods of today, but which, in the absence of any contradictory evidence, were perfectly adequate for the times.

The simplest scenario for a flat Earth is that the world goes on forever. This causes problems for the sun, moon and stars, but add a convenient underground cavern for them to pass through and the theory has been satisfactorily patched up. My personal favourite mythology is an ancient eastern Indian one in which the Earth rested on the backs of four great elephants. These in turn stood on the back of an even larger turtle which, in its turn, swam in a boundless, bottomless ocean. This hypothesis encompasses an intriguing shift from an infinite land to an infinite sea. In a sense, though, we do float in an 'infinite' sea – except that our sea is one of near-vacuum, rather than of matter. As we now know, infinite, or even merely large, amounts of matter is not a stable proposition. Yet one branch of modern physics proposes that there is indeed a limitless ocean of matter flowing just below the surface of the universe. The development of the microchip rests, or perhaps I should say floats, upon this and related theories.

In classical Newtonian physics, an object's energy was simply half the product of its mass and its velocity squared. As mass was always a positive quantity (as is any real quantity squared), the energy too had to be positive. As usual, in relativistic Einsteinian physics the situation is a little more complicated. The total energy of an object is now known to be comprised of the energy equivalent of its rest mass (m_0c^2), and the energy due to its motion ($m_0cv\gamma$); though not simply their addition. Instead, the total energy is the square root of the sum of their squares (see Fig. 10.1) This results from the invariance of four-momentum (see Appendix C). For small velocities the energy due to motion closely approximates that given by Newtonian mechanics, as usual.

When taking any square root, we can choose either the positive or negative value of the result; both 2^2 and $(-2)^2$ yield 4. Taking the positive value yields the energy of all normal matter, composed, as it is, of positive energy electrons, protons, neutrons and so on. But there is no reason not to take the negative value. This is precisely what the twentieth-century English physicist Dirac did, and he came to the startling conclusion that there should exist matter which possesses a negative mass-energy. This result has several interesting consequences, some of which at least could be tested. But before we go on to discuss these, we need to know a little more about energy.

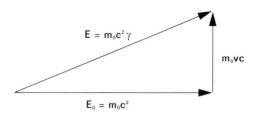

$$E = m_0c^2\gamma$$

$$m_0vc$$

$$E_0 = m_0c^2$$

Fig. 10.1 The total energy of an object.

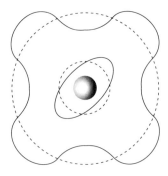

Fig. 10.2 Standing electron waves on a circle form the electron orbits.

Energy

All objects possess energy – no energy no object, nothing. Also, any object, given the opportunity, will tend to relax into the lowest available energy state. Just as water flows downhill and fills hollows, so too do electrons 'flow' towards protons, filling the lowest energy states available. These are both examples of entropy in action. As we saw in Chapter 9, on the small scale the universe's discrete nature manifests itself. One consequence of this is that electrons can only orbit nuclei at various discrete radii. This results directly from the dual wave-particle nature of matter. As electrons have a characteristic wavelength, only an integral number of these waves can lie in any electron orbit (see Fig. 10.2). This prevents the electrons 'falling' into the nucleus, as one wavelength is the length of the smallest circumference at which an electron can orbit. At least they cannot do so under normal conditions, for, as we saw earlier, under the extreme conditions of a neutron star there is no space between the atoms in which to orbit, and the electrons are 'compressed' into adjacent nuclei. We shall ignore these extremes, and concentrate on matter under the conditions in which we usually encounter it. These nuclear electrons therefore can only possess discrete energies relative to a nucleus, corresponding to these discrete orbits.

Now the laws of nature are such that only two electrons can occupy the lowest energy state associated with a single wavelength. This exclusion principle is similar to the rules of the 'game' in our entropy model of Chapter 9. Similarly, only eight electrons can fit in the next energy level – and so on, with more fitting in each level.

BOTTOMLESS SEAS, LIMITLESS WELLS

Wave number   Total energy (eV)

∞ ———————— Continuum ———————— $m_e c^2$

3 ———————————————————— $m_e c^2 - 1.5$

2 ———————————————————— $m_e c^2 - 3.4$

1 ———————————————————— $m_e c^2 - 13.6$

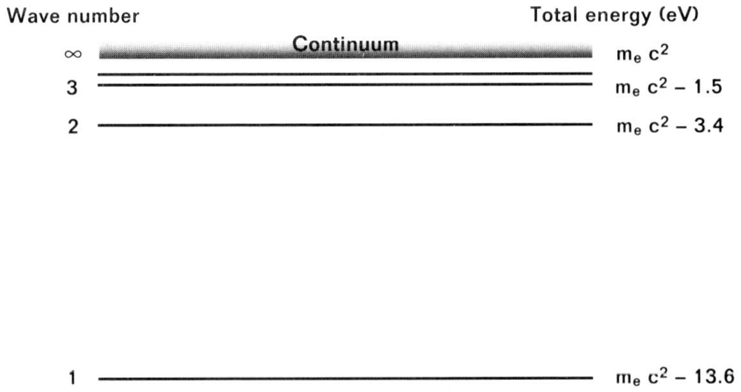

Fig. 10.3 Electron energy levels, and the number of waves in each orbit, in the hydrogen atom.

Successively higher energy levels also get closer together – in other words, the higher the electron goes, the less energy it takes to climb from one level to the next (see Fig. 10.3). There is no upper limit to these levels. Although the speed of light is a barrier to velocity, it represents an infinite amount of energy for any object of finite rest mass. In addition, the uppermost layer has the capacity to contain an infinite number of orbiting electrons.

As mentioned above, due to entropy all things tend to sink to the lowest available energy levels. Consequently, electrons naturally tend to fill energy levels from the bottom up. The exclusion principle prevents all electrons flowing into the lowest level, and dictates the filling sequence of atoms with greater numbers of electrons. It is this filling up of lower energy levels that gives rise to a large part of the chemical properties of different atoms, but that is another branch of science entirely and one that I do not intend tackling in this book. (Interested readers can learn about the origins of the periodic table in any of the hundreds of excellent chemistry books that are available.)

Negative energy
The existence of Dirac's negative energy introduces levels below zero. Symmetry dictates that these will mirror the positive ones (see Fig. 10.4). Similarly, these levels will obey all the usual exclusion principles, etc.. What follows is something similar to the reasoning of Dirac.

As everything tends to relax into the lowest energy state available, we should expect all normal matter to drop down into the negative energy states. That it has not done so already indicates that these states are full. We shall be looking at the implications of this shortly; for now we will accept, as Dirac did, that this is true. Suppose, then, that sufficient energy is supplied to a negative energy particle – a negative energy electron, for instance – to lift it into a 'normal' positive energy state. This would leave a hole in the negative energy state that will subsequently be available for a normal electron to fall into. As the other negative energy electrons are free to move, just as positive energy ones are, the hole will move also. It will then look like a particle in its own right. Now when a normal electron falls into this hole, or equivalently when an electron and a hole collide, it will disappear, and energy will be released in the form of electromagnetic radiation. The energy will be identical to that required to lift the negative energy electron out of the original hole. Now, electromagnetic radiation possesses no charge. Consequently, the hole must have had an equal and opposite charge to that of the electron, so that when the two are combined there is zero net charge. This argument also holds for the other properties of an electron; for example the hole must have the opposite spin to an electron. In every sense then, the hole is an anti-electron. Because of its positive charge, it is also referred to as a positron.

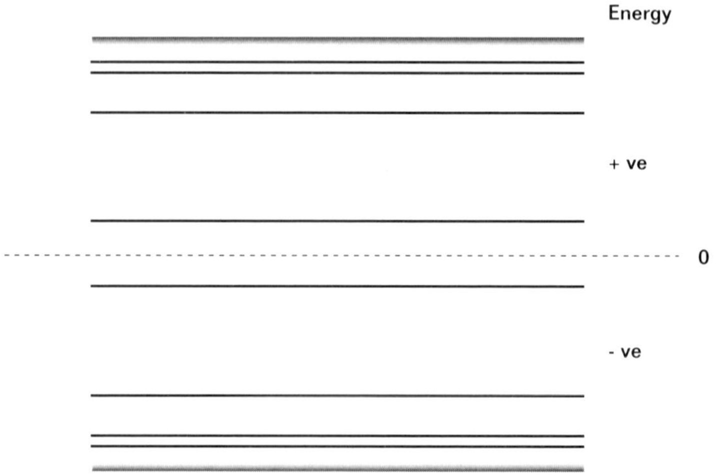

Fig. 10.4 Negative energy levels mirror positive ones.

This may seem a very tenuous argument, but such was Dirac's repu-
tation that contemporary scientists began to search for these
hypothetical anti-electrons in high-energy collisions, where sufficient
energies ($2\,m_e\,c^2$ where m_e is the rest mass of an electron) are produced
to create such electron-positron, anti-particle pairs. Undoubtedly to
many scientists' surprise, such anti-particle pairs were found and
Dirac's theory of negative energies was vindicated.

Since then other anti-particles, anti-protons, anti-neutrons and so
on have been observed. Subsequently, the more fundamental quantum and gauge theories have been shown to lead to the same conclusions regarding the existence of negative energy particles, though
without any tacit reference to holes.

There is a major problem associated with this theory of negative
energies. In order for there to be any positive energy electrons – that is,
to explain why they have not all long ago sunk to lower, negative
energy levels, Dirac had to assume that all the negative energy levels
were full. But there are an infinite number of these levels representing
energies down to minus infinity, a level that itself can contain an infinite number of negative energy electrons. If we assume that the lowest
level is not full, there is nothing to prevent electrons from higher
energy levels dropping down into them and, incidentally, radiating
infinite amounts of energy. This in turn would leave our universe full
of Dirac holes, which every normal electron will want to fall into.

We are left, then, with the same conclusion as Dirac, that all the
negative energy levels must be full. Yet this requires an infinite
amount of matter. So far we have only considered negative energy
electrons. The same reasoning applies to other, heavier particles such
as protons and neutrons, some of which have also been discovered.
But this is largely irrelevant! Infinite is infinite – multiply it by 2000 in
going from the mass of an electron to that of a proton, and it is still as
large as ever.

Must we accept then that our universe does indeed float on an infinite sea of matter, albeit negative? Well, where there is matter, there is
also gravity. And, with an infinite amount of matter, the gravity must
also, necessarily, be infinite. This is similar to the situation we encountered in Olbers' paradox. So why are we not crushed by the infinite
gravitational forces involved? That this matter possesses negative
mass-energy only makes the problem more complicated. For we must
also ask another question: what sort of gravitational interaction might
we expect with negative mass-energy? Does it attract or repel positive

matter? Even a finite amount of such matter will produce a gravitational field. That we cannot detect any anomalous gravitational effects poses a serious objection to Dirac's conception of matter in negative energy states. And there is another problem with this idea – our inability directly to observe matter in its negative energy state. We can detect the hole left behind when a particle is raised to a positive energy state, yet we are unable to observe it before its rise; nor can we observe a particle after it has dropped into a hole. But this is a minor problem compared to that of an infinite gravitational background. Ideally, we would like a solution that deals with all these problems.

By now it should come as no surprise that the solution involves matter travelling backwards in time.

Reverse time

Consider the situation from the point of view of a reverse time observer, which we will assume corresponds to a condition of negative energy. By definition, to him everything on his side of zero energy is positive. For him it is we who are travelling backwards in time, we who have negative energy. Now, in his time frame electrons naturally tend to occupy the lowest available energy levels – those closest to zero energy. There is certainly no requirement for every energy level above the lowest to be occupied, any more than there is in our time frame. But what are higher positive energy levels for him are lower negative ones for us. Adopting this hypothesis, we do not need to postulate infinitely filled, infinite negative energy wells. For the laws of entropy operate to fill the energy levels closest to zero on both sides of the energy barrier.

The fact that some energy levels are vacant, even some of the lowest ones in the sense of being nearer zero, should not concern us too much. For, as we saw in Chapter 5, there can be no – or perhaps we should say very little – communication between positive and negative time/energy domains, and so we cannot detect any such vacant 'holes'. This resolves not only the problem of an infinite gravity, but also the problem of our inability to observe any gravity associated with even a finite amount of negative energy. It also accounts for our inability to observe negative energy matter directly.

Consequently, the positrons we observe are not electron holes, with all the attendant problems associated with infinite wells, which Dirac proposed. Instead, a positron is simply an electron in another of the four states in which gauge theory predicts it can exist. In the light of the above arguments the four states are the electron itself, the positron, and their negative energy, reverse time, counterparts. (The full mathematical development of the gauge theory that gives rise to these four states is beyond the scope of this book, being largely a matter for postgraduate study, and it is to texts of this level that any interested readers are directed. However, the identification of two of these states with negative energy and reverse time will not be found in the books currently available, since travel backwards in time is still widely regarded as impossible.)

Energy and temperature

One further property associated with energy, and also with entropy, is temperature. We are all familiar with hot and cold. In water, for example, the molecules are hurtling about, loosely connected to the whole. Add energy to these and they will rush about more vigorously. Continue adding energy and eventually there comes a point at which the molecules will break completely free of the attractive forces of their neighbours, and rush apart. They have then become a gas. Obviously, the water has been heated. Raising the temperature then, is identical with adding energy. Alternatively, removing energy will cause the molecules to slow down. Eventually, if we continue removing energy, the mutual attraction between molecules will lock them in position relative to their neighbours. At this point we have a solid, ice. But even in such a solid the molecules are still moving: they oscillate in all three directions about a fixed point in the lattice formed with their fellows. Removing energy, then, results in a reduction of the temperature. Temperature is in fact, directly related to the average energy of the particles in an object.

More specifically, temperature is related to the average intermolecular energy; the energy associated with the net motion is not involved. To see this consider the following simplified example. Suppose the average intermolecular speed of the molecules in a stone is 10 m/s. Naturally, this has a certain temperature associated with it, whose actual value is not important. Now suppose we throw the stone at 10 m/s, what is its temperature? Obviously, the same; though not exactly, as we shall see shortly. So although the average velocity of the molecules relative to us has increased, the temperature has not. Alternatively, if we heated the stone until the average intermolecular speed was 20 m/s it would obviously have a higher temperature.

The more energy we extract, the lower the temperature and hence the internal energy. Extracting more heat energy from a solid results in a reduction of the oscillations within the lattice. Eventually, when sufficient energy has been removed, the molecules will become absolutely motionless. However, the intrinsic energy of the rest mass (m_0c^2) remains. So even perfectly static matter has a finite, actually very large, positive energy. Consequently, it still has a positive temperature associated with it.

As we saw earlier, there exists a mirror image universe of negative energy, reverse time matter, coincident with the positive energy universe we inhabit. From the above description of temperature it is obvious that matter in this reverse time universe must possess negative temperatures. So could we lower the temperature of an object in our universe enough to make it reverse in time?

Relativistic thermodynamics

If we could directly observe the intermolecular motion in the stone of our example above, we could deduce its temperature. When it was moving relative to us, time dilation would cause all motions to slow. Therefore, we would observe a reduction of the average intermolecular speed, and calculate a lower temperature than for a stone at rest relative to us. At higher relative velocities, the time dilation is greater and the corresponding temperatures lower. Finally, at the speed of light all motion would cease, and so at the light (time) barrier the temperature would be zero. Beyond this, it is reasonable to expect the temperature to be lower still, below zero. The answer to the question posed above, then, is yes – move an object fast enough (FTL) and the temperature will fall below zero.

So the view of reverse time that arose in connection with the macroscopic physical theories of special and general relativity, and again with black holes and the ultimate fate of the universe, has risen yet again. This time it is in connection with the theories of fundamental particle physics, and with such commonplace ideas as temperature. It is almost as if the harder the idea of reverse time is suppressed in one area, the more persistently it re-emerges elsewhere. This is often the way with new ideas which contradict our old ones. Struggle as we may against these unfamiliar concepts, ultimately we must accept the obvious. Travel backwards in time is indeed possible. There are even ways for a human being to reverse his or her direction in time – difficult though they are, in that they involve a 1 g acceleration for a proper year, or falling into a galactic black hole. But these are technological problems. In theory, at least, we can move both ways in time.

XI

All Physics Is Geometry

*Philosophy is written in this grand book – I mean the uni-
verse – which stands continually open to our gaze, but it
cannot be understood unless one first learns to comprehend the language and interpret the characters in which it
is written. It is written in the language of mathematics,
and its characters are triangles, circles, and other geomet-
rical figures, without which it is humanly impossible to
understand a single word; without these, one is wandering
about in a dark labyrinth.*

Galileo Galilei

Let's now take a fresh look at some of the examples given in previous
chapters. To start with, let's consider length contraction and time dilation in terms of four-space geometry. As we have seen, we can ignore
the two spatial dimensions in which there is no relative motion. This
not only simplifies the mathematics but also allows us to draw two-
dimensional diagrams with relative ease. There are diagrams of four-
dimensional objects, and there are even computer programs that allow
you to rotate them, colour the surfaces and explore them. These are
both instructional and entertaining, if somewhat mind-boggling. But
for our purposes two dimensions will be sufficient.

Motion
Consider again the case where you and I are moving at a relative velocity of $\frac{3}{4}$c towards each other, in identical spacecraft. As we saw earlier, I
will appear only 66 per cent as long to you, in the direction of motion,
as I do to myself. Also, things will appear to you to take 51 per cent
longer to occur aboard my spacecraft than they do for me. I will come
to the same conclusions regarding lengths and events on board your
craft. Alternatively, if you and I were to measure the four-space length

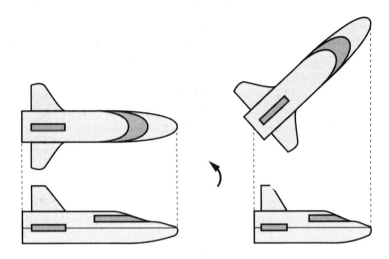

Fig. 11.1 The apparent contraction of a rotated object.

of anything on board either craft or anywhere else we would both arrive at the same result because four-space length is an invariant the same for all observers.

Now consider the case where our two spacecraft are not in relative motion, but at rest and rotated with respect to each other (see Fig. 11.1). If you were to measure the length of my craft in the direction that yours is facing it would be shorter than usual; in fact, at an angle of 41°, it would be exactly 66 per cent of the length of your craft. If we were to take the square root of the sum of the squares of this length, and the perpendicular one, you would arrive at the original length. One way of looking at this is that part of the length in one direction has been rotated into the other direction, and vice versa for lengths that were in this other direction to start with. This is exactly analogous to what occurs during relative motion in space-time. Some of the length, in the direction of motion, is rotated into the time direction, and some of the time is rotated into one spatial direction.

If we continue rotating our spacecraft, eventually what was in your x direction will be transformed into my y and vice versa. Similarly, in space-time there is a point, at the speed of light, at which one length and time exchange places. Relativistic motion forwards or backwards is analogous to rotation in one direction or the other. (A word of warning: the actual mathematics of space-time are a little more complex than those for Euclidean rotation, in that they involve purely imaginary angles. I do not propose to go into this here, but the equations for the Lorentz transformation as a rotation are given in Appendix D.)

One consequence of this geometric interpretation is a justification of the substitution of a 'pseudo' sub-light velocity into the Lorentz equations when the light barrier is breached. Both pseudo and normal sub-light velocities are projections on the same axis. And just as the function sin θ in the case of rotation produces the same projection for a pair of angles, one below and one above 90°, so too do the same pseudo and normal sub-light velocities.

Incidentally, as objects approach the speed of light there is an additional apparent rotation when viewed from the side. This is due to a combination of the contraction of the length in the direction of motion, and the time delay between the arrival of light from the back of the object and the front. At high speed this latter is a significant fraction of the time for the object to move through its own length. Here I shall break my own rule regarding recommendations just long enough to direct the interested reader to some excellent computer simulations of this apparent rotation in *Inside Relativity* by Mook and Vargish (see Bibliography). Remember that this additional rotation is an apparent one in three-space, for the views from in front and behind remain unchanged, unlike the situation for real rotation.

Time dilation

We have already discussed the mathematics and physical verification of time dilation, and we have investigated the geometry of four spacetime. But time dilation is so fundamental, and yet so removed from everyday experience, that it is worth approaching from yet another direction, a wholly geometric one.

We will enlist the aid of our old friend the flatlander, sending him on one of his triangular journeys. This time, though, we shall get him to push an object ahead of him, asking him to be sure that he does not rotate it as he changes direction. So that we can be sure that he does not cheat we will issue him with an arrow, which we can follow clearly. First, we will conduct this experiment in a purely flat, Euclidean space. As can be seen in Fig. 11.2, when our flatlander has completed his circuit and is back at his starting point the arrow realigns perfectly with its original position. In fact the object will always realign perfectly, however large the triangle is and whatever angles we choose for it.

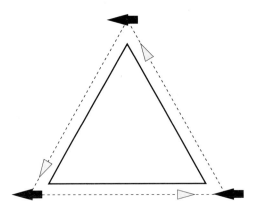

Fig. 11.2 An object taken on a closed circuit in flat, Euclidean space.

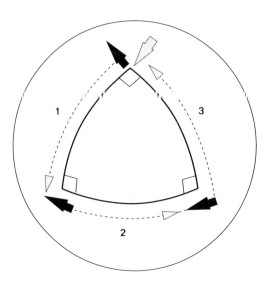

Fig. 11.3 The rotation of an object embedded in the curved surface space of a sphere when it is taken on a closed circuit (1–2–3).

Now we will ask him to conduct the same experiment in a two-dimensional space embedded in the surface of a sphere, and travel for a full quarter of a great arc in each direction (see Fig. 11.3). At the end of the circuit the object he has pushed is rotated 90° relative to its original orientation. Yet relative to his space, our flatlander has not turned the object at any point of the journey. The rotation results entirely from the curvature of the space in which it, and he, are embedded.

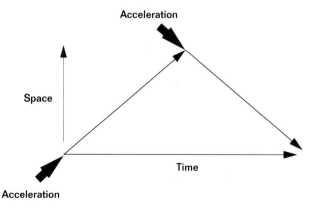

Fig. 11.4 The courses of stationary and moving observers in space–time.

The amount of rotation is dependent on the length of the journey: shorter trips result in less rotation, longer ones in more. For a sphere the rotation is equal to the solid angle subtended by the area contained within the circuit. This is generally true for any closed path, however circuitous the route – I chose a triangle with equal sides one quarter the circumference in length to simplify the illustration. Generally, for all curved spaces, travelling in a closed circuit results in a rotation of the object.

In four-space-time that rotation cannot be expected to be simply spatial. Consequently, when we return to our starting point after a journey we might intuitively expect our clock to disagree with that of someone who has remained at our point of origin. In four-space the stationary observer is only moving in the time domain, while we have also moved in space (see Fig. 11.4). It is the act of acceleration in three-space (equivalent to rotation in four-space-time) that causes our departure from this straight time line. Viewed in this way, time dilation is inevitable in a curved space-time

The twin paradox
Suppose we take two twins, Cain and Abel, and send them up a mountain from the same starting point. The first, Cain, we send straight up. At the same time we send the second, Abel, on a trail that zig-zags up. When they meet at the top they are both the same distance from the start of their journey, yet one has travelled a greater distance than the other. The one who travelled the shorter distance scaled a steeper incline than his brother. The difference in the paths of

the two brothers lies in the way in which the journey is undertaken. It is similar for our space-travelling twins of Chapter 2. The one who underwent the most acceleration would have arrived back having travelled through a shorter length of proper time than his brother. By undergoing acceleration, one of them has zig-zagged through space-time. In one case the second twin negotiated a less steep incline, and in the other case less time.

The changes in direction, as Abel walked up the mountain, took place over very short distances. For the most part he was travelling in a straight line, just like his brother. The same is true for the space-farer. He too accelerates for only short times, and spends most of the time in constant relative motion. Yet it is these small accelerations that determine for whom the effects of the journey accumulate.

Motion in space-time really is a problem in geometry. Dynamic problems in three dimensions become static, geometric ones in four. And frequently, as we have seen, we can reduce the dimensions to two with a suitable choice of coordinate axes – that is, one which aligns with one of the coordinate axes the direction of motion.

Gravity

We can define gravity as the field of force in space produced by the presence of mass. Alternatively, mass produces a distortion of space-time. In a very real sense space-time is curved by the presence of matter. The paths of objects in the presence of this distortion trace out curves in four-space-time.

In a flat, Euclidean space the shortest distance between two points is a straight line. In a curved space this is no longer true. This may be a difficult idea to grasp at first. Let's look in on our flatlander friend embedded in the surface of a sphere, and ask him what the shortest distance between two points is. A straight line in three dimensions strays outside his universe, and therefore does not exist for him. His 'straight' line must lie entirely within his space. What, then, is the shortest distance between two points (the geodesic) for our flatlander who cannot leave the surface of a sphere? The answer (see Fig. 11.5) is the arc of a great circle – that is, part of the circumference of a circle whose centre is that of the sphere. Remember the example of the flight from London to San Francisco in Chapter 6? The geodesics for a flat, Euclidean, space are, of course, our familiar straight lines; for the surface of a sphere, great arcs; and in four-space-time, the paths followed by electromagnetic waves.

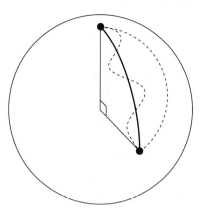

Fig. 11.5 The shortest distance or geodesic between two points of the surface of a sphere.

We are normally unaware of the curvature of our space-time, because we are so small in comparison with this curvature. A flat-lander would find it difficult to determine the curvature of his space over small distances. Yet, as we have seen, when he performs the same experiment over a significant fraction of the circumference the curvature becomes all too apparent. As we saw earlier, if he starts at any point; moves through one quarter of an arc; turns left and again moves through one quarter of an arc; and finally repeats the process yet again, he will have returned to the start of his journey, having circumnavigated a three-right-angled triangle. Over that distance the gradual curvature of the sphere will have produced a large cumulative effect. The curvature of our space-time due to the presence of mass is small, at least thankfully so in our neighbourhood. Yet place something in orbit for sufficient time and the discrepancies in duration will accumulate. Not surprisingly, this is also analogous to what happens with relative motion. Move a little distance and space-time seems the same for both of us; or, more correctly, the differences are too small to measure. Move a long way and come back and our clocks are noticeably different, due to the cumulative effect on the curvature of your space-time during your entire journey.

Gauge theory
One of the first attempts to unify all the forces of nature into one coherent theory, gauge theory introduces a geometric distortion of

space-time due to the presence of electric charge, in exactly the same way that general relativity introduces curvature due to the presence of mass. (I do not propose to introduce the entire mathematical formalism here, as I have deliberately limited the mathematics in this book to what could reasonably be understood by those who have undergone schooling until their late teens in most of the world's educational institutions. And the mathematics required for even a moderate understanding of gauge theory is considerably above that, requiring a degree-level education in either mathematics or one of the classical sciences.)

Gauge theory is important because it is a fairly successful attempt to represent the other forces of nature as geometric distortions in the continuum. It also succeeds in partially bridging the gap between Einstein's classical theories of relativity and modern quantum theory, giving rise to several of the results presented earlier in this book – for example, Dirac's positive and negative energy particles. Finally, gauge theory forms a useful starting point for the search for theories with which to unify all the forces of nature into a single coherent whole, though these appear to require more than our by now familiar four dimensions.

· XII ·
The Fifth Dimension and the Multiverse

When you have eliminated the impossible, whatever is left,
no matter how improbable, is the answer.

Sir Arthur Conan Doyle's character, Sherlock Holmes,
on the philosophy of the scientific method

The evidence for travel in both directions in time exists in special relativity, general relativity and thermodynamics, and generally throughout the physical sciences. Without reverse time travel there are considerable philosophical and theoretical difficulties, such as that posed by Dirac's multiple infinite negative mass-energy background. Conversely, the only objection is that posed by the causality paradox with which this book opened.

Time travel has been most extensively investigated in connection with Schwartzchild wormholes. In Chapter 7 we saw how these linked different space-time continuums. Alternatively, it has been proposed that in a curved space-time they could link different points in the same continuum. The two continuums in Fig. 7.9 would then be connected. Yet this wormhole connects not simply distant points in the same space, but points in the space-time. This allows for the possibility of using a wormhole to travel to a previous time in the same universe, which puts us at liberty to interfere with our personal histories – with all the paradoxes that this entails. So how have wormhole investigators dealt with this objection?

The cosmic censor
One approach, adopted by Professor Hawking and by others, has been to invoke a cosmic censor, an omnipotent entity that intervenes to prevent the occurrence of a paradox. It operates something like this. If a man goes back in time and attempts to alter his personal history, for

example by trying to kill his father then the cosmic censor would have it that the murdered man was not really his father. There can always be an element of doubt with paternity. A similar objection can be raised if the time traveller were to kill his mother: he could, for instance, have been adopted. But what if he attempts to commit a form of retrograde suicide by killing his earlier self? Presumably in this kind of situation the cosmic censor takes a more active role, depending on the method employed. If, for example, the time traveller elects to shoot his earlier self, then the gun will misfire or the bullet will simply miss.

The cosmic censor, then, ensures that any and every attempt by the time traveller to alter his personal history will be frustrated. Consequently, if he attempts to communicate with his earlier self in any way he will only be able to do so if he already did, and then only in exactly that way. This would imply an absolute deterministic universe, a classical view that is very much contrary to the tenets of modern, probabilistic quantum theory.

Following Sherlock Holmes' exhortation, we are left with the alternative presented earlier: that a wormhole conveys us to a completely different universe, one that is completely divorced from our personal history. Perhaps, then, travelling back in time always involves a shift into another universe. And why just two universes? If we plunge into another black hole in this new universe we cannot return to our old universe, for then we would be faced with the possibility of encountering our earlier self. This implies that there is a whole series of four-dimensional space-time continuums. Yet where are these other universes? They cannot be anywhere else in space or time. There is nowhere in space-time that they can be, for each universe occupies a complete four-dimensional continuum.

The fifth dimension

Why four dimensions? Well, there have to be at least four. For instance, this book requires four dimensions – three to occupy and one in which to have been written. This simple example represents what is known as the anthropic principle. Basically, this states that things are as they are, otherwise neither you, nor I, nor this book would exist in the exact form that they do. Another way of looking at it is that the past is immutable; once an event has happened, all the probabilities are zero except for the actual eventualities that occurred, for which the probabilities are one. Things happened as they did because they must have in order for us to be here; we're here because, we're here because, we're here because, we're here ... and so on. One consequence of this is that four dimensions are necessary.

But why should there not be more dimensions; five, six, seven – or forty-eight? There is no reason whatsoever to limit ourselves to four, and a great deal to be gained by assuming more. This is not a new idea, and scientists have used it to make significant progress towards constructing a fully unified theory of nature. Currently, the most popular candidate is super string theory, which requires ten dimensions. For our present purposes we will explore the consequences of just five. First, why five?

Let's return one final time to the 'paradox' of the father killed by his own son. We have already postulated that the murder would take place in an alternative universe – that is, at the same place where, and time when, the murder did not occur; not somewhere else or somewhen else, but at some what-if else, in an alternative reality that has the same four-space-time coordinates, but not a fifth. In five dimensions we can finally lay to rest our paradox as follows. The man travels back in time. In so doing he enters the reverse time, mirror image, of our universe. When he starts moving forwards in time again, the same direction as ourselves, he is in an alternative universe. There he is at liberty to kill the man who would have fathered not him, but his alternative in that universe. There is no paradox; his father, unmurdered, inhabits an entirely different universe, some distance in the fifth dimension from the one in which the murder is committed.

The time traveller is even at liberty to murder himself. For it is another earlier self that he kills. In so doing he has not interfered in any way with his personal history, for that has occurred in another time line, one from which he has forever vanished. If there is a cosmic censor, his task now is simply to prevent time travellers getting back to their home universes.

There is further support for this solution. In the neighbourhood of wormholes, probability is not conserved. In our single universe the sum of the probabilities for all outcomes of a particular event, or series of events, is one. Toss a coin and there is a 50 per cent (0.5) chance it will land head up and 50 per cent (0.5) tails. One and only one outcome is certain. After the event the probabilities reduce to one for the actual outcome (the coin lands tails up, say) and zero for all others (head up). Both before and after, the probabilities sum to one, they are conserved. After passing through a wormhole this is no longer true.

The probabilities can now add to more than one. The coin could simultaneously land both head and tails up. This requires the existence of two coins, one in each of two alternative universes.

Now a fifth dimension results in not just two but a whole series of alternative realities, each representing a different quantum possibility in some hyper- (at least five-) dimensional multiverse, and consequently each different from its neighbour. This difference increases with increasing distance in the fifth dimension, in the same way in which the environment varies with either space or time. For example, look out of a window pane. Now look at the adjacent view through the next. There is a difference in what you see, a difference between the environment in the one area and the next. Even were you glancing at a section of lawn, the grass in adjacent areas is subtly different. Similarly, if you look at the same scene at different times it will also be different. The section of lawn will have grown, or the wind may have rearranged the blades of grass. Just as the amount of variation depends on many factors for the four dimensions of space-time, so too does it in the fifth dimension. It may be that adjacent universes differ by only a single quantum displacement. Alternatively, they may be so different that we have never existed in them, completely frustrating our time travelling, alternative patricide.

I believe that the arguments presented in this book provide a convincing case for the existence of time travel. Time is simply another typical, if very large, dimension. To avoid the obvious paradoxes involved in travel in the fourth dimension we require the existence of a fifth; and why not? If super string theory represents a deeper understanding of reality, then perhaps there are actually ten dimensions. Five, ten or more, the universe is even bigger than we imagined. By now this should not be at all surprising.

At each new insight into the nature of reality, man has had to expand his horizons: from a flat Earth bounded by the extent of the Nile valley, to a round Earth at the centre of a shell on which the stars were fixed; on to a planet orbiting the sun, to a typical stellar system, one amongst many in the Milky Way; on further, to a universe containing a myriad of galaxies, to clusters of galaxies forming super-clusters. And now our horizons must expand again, from just one universe to one amongst an 'infinite' set of alternatives. Now infinity is a useful mathematical term, but just as the three-dimensional universe is curved back on itself to form a finite, albeit almightily large, volume, so too is the four-dimensional continuum of space-time curved in five dimensions, resulting in a finite temporal extent. What, then, of the fifth dimension? Might it also be curved in yet another higher dimension? Again, why not?

Life, the multiverse and everything

In this book we have built up the following coherent, and self-consistent, picture of the universe. The universe began 15,000 million years ago. It is a massive white hole expanding out from a single point in four-dimensional space-time. In the simplest model it is a hypersphere, the radius of which is time and the surface our familiar three-dimensional space. At the present time the radius, which is 15 million light years, is so large that locally space appears almost flat. On this scale, an ant on the surface of a still pond would have a better chance of detecting the curvature of the Earth in the bending of the water beneath it than we have of detecting the curvature of the universe. This vast four-dimensional balloon is still expanding, yet it remains within its Schwartzchild radius. Throughout the surface, blue-lipped, black holes are nibbling away at the very fabric of space-time, growing ever larger and more voracious. At some point in the far distant future (the end of time) these will join into one vast hole, and the arrow of time, which currently points outwards, will turn inwards. The universe will collapse back along a parallel time line.

Subsequently, the universe will pass through the singularity at its centre to emerge at another point in the fifth dimension. In so doing it will form an alternative forward-moving universe. And so on, generating the multitude of universes that comprise the cosmos, for want of a better term. Now if the cosmos is indeed infinite in the fifth dimension then we can reason, as was done at the beginning of Chapter 2, that all possibilities, no matter how improbable, must occur – that in some universe you are emperor of the Earth, in another emperor of the universe. For you must exist in an infinite subset of universes, and if you divide infinity by any number it is still infinite. So surely there is a universe in which you are unique, in that you exist only there and in no other universe. But this is true only if you exist in an infinite number of universes! So we arrive at a new paradox. All this really tells us this that we should always beware of infinities. I would hazard that this means that the cosmos is finite in the fifth dimension, just as it was in the previous four – though it is always dangerous to discount something just on the basis of a paradox, especially as we have other higher dimensions to call upon.

The closing of the circle

Let's look again at that most fascinating of space-time-what-if points, the singularity at the beginning and end of every universe. I am going to postulate a five-dimensional model; it will be the simplest one I can think of – a five-dimensional sphere. Let's drop two space dimensions and curve time through the fifth dimension. Imagine the remaining spatial dimension as a circle expanding on a sphere, the radius of which is the fifth dimension (see Fig. 12.1). Time now lies along great arcs emanating from a single point on the sphere – the white hole origin. Three-space forms the surface volume of a hypersphere, the radius of which is also now curved in a higher dimension. On this diagram the circle represents the extent of one spatial dimension of the universe at a particular moment in time. In this simplest symmetric model, the other two spatial dimensions are of identical shape and size but in directions that we cannot depict. This representative circle expands with time until it reaches the circumference of the fifth-dimensional sphere. It then begins to contract, shrinking back to a point.

As an analogy, imagine a planet composed entirely of water. A wave starts at one pole, which we shall arbitrarily label the north. As the circular wave flows around the globe it spreads out, expanding as it

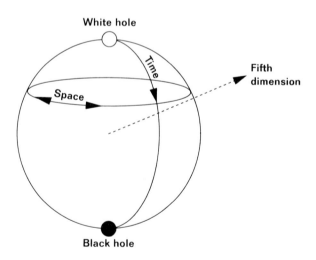

Fig. 12.1 A symmetric, five-dimensional model of a hypersphere.

approaches the equator. As it expands its amplitude decreases as the energy is spread over a wider front. Once it passes the equator it begins to contract, collapsing back to the south pole. As it does so, the amplitude builds back up to the intensity it had at the north pole, assuming conservation of energy. Once the south pole is reached the wave does not vanish, but passes through itself and goes round again. Note that different cycles, while they occupy the same space, do not occupy the same space-time – that is, no two waves occur at the same time. Of course the real universe has more dimensions, and the repetition occurs at the same time, but at a different what-if.

This five-dimensional hyperspherical model, then, answers the questions posed in earlier chapters as to when, and why, the universe changes from its white hole to its black hole state. The theory discussed earlier assumed a flat, Euclidean four-space-time. This resulted in the transition from one state to the other occurring only after an infinite time. In a curved, fifth-dimensional cosmos the transition occurs naturally at the point of maximum four-radius. However, how we would measure the five-dimensional curvature, and hence the life expectancy, of the universe, I do not know. This does not mean, however, that it cannot be done, though the four-dimensional curvature has yet to be measured with any degree of accuracy.

Continuing with our simple spherical model, at the end of the cycle, the circle will contract back to a single point. Here all space-time, matter-energy flows through the 'singularity', and then back out, on the surface of a second sphere. And so we have a set of spheres nested within one another, a five-dimensional onion (see Fig. 12.2). This 'onion' model I owe to Stephen Hawking's *A Brief History of Time*. It is a simple, elegant model of the process of rebirth in a fifth dimension. The singularity is no longer quite as ferocious as it was in four dimensions. In particular, if there is any net rotation in the universe then, as we have seen, the singularity will form a ring. Space-time, matter-energy will flow through this hole in the ring with even greater facility than through a point. The model still holds. This is, as I have said, the simplest model. As we have no way of determining the nature of the actual five-curvature, it is as good as any, and serves to account for at least some details of our black–white hole universe.

The size of the universe

How big, then, is the universe? By this I mean: what is the three-volume? Well, this depends on which of the models we use. For the

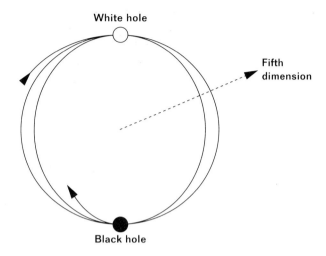

Fig. 12.2 Alternative universes stacked successively in the fifth dimension.

simplest model, an exploding sphere in a flat three-space, the volume is $\frac{4}{3}\pi\,(c\tau)^3$ (the volume of a simple three-sphere), where τ is the proper time since the beginning of this cycle (the age of the universe).

For the four-dimensional hyperspherical model, where time represents the radius and space the surface shell that expands out from it, the universe simply occupies this surface volume. For a four-dimensional hypersphere this is $2\pi^2\,(c\tau)^3$, almost five times that of the simple three-sphere. This is to be expected: it arises in a similar way to that in which the surface area of a sphere ($4\,\pi\,r^2$) exceeds that of a circle ($\pi\,r^2$). This increased volume has significant implications for the estimates of the total mass of the universe.

For the five-dimensional hyperspherical model, our familiar three-space forms a ring volume on the four-dimensional surface. By dropping two of the space dimensions, as we did above, we can determine the four-dimensional radius at any moment in time. The volume is then

$$2\pi^2\left(R\,\sin\left(\frac{c\tau}{R}\right)\right)^3$$

where R is the radius of the five-dimensional hypersphere. At present we have no way of determining this radius, though if we were able to measure the volume at one moment in time we could calculate its value for all time. This, if we accept the five-dimensional model, would in turn tell us for how much longer the universe will expand. In this model, the expansion of the universe is no longer linear. Initially, such a universe expands as if it were a four-hypersphere. In time, the rate of expansion decreases until, at time T_e of maximum size

$$\left(\frac{16\,(cT_e)^3}{\pi} \right)$$

it ceases altogether. At this point the volume of the universe would be only 1.2 times that of a three-sphere expanding at the speed of light for the same time.

Generally, the geometry of the universe in five-space determines its three-space volume at all moments in time.

Space travel

What, then, of our prospects for travel in the universe at large? Well, if we are happy to crawl around below the speed of light we can get to anywhere within the universe in just under two years. On our return, however, we would find that a tremendous time has passed for those we left behind. FTL is possible, but if we do not want to risk killing our own fathers we would be wise to arrange to come back after we had left. But when we emerge from FTL, will we not be in another universe? Yes, but this may present no problem. For if it is similar to our own, in that up to the point of our departure we have a common history, then neither we, nor the inhabitants of this new universe, will ever detect the difference.

In order truly to conquer space we must conquer space-time. To do this we must be willing to deal with the fifth dimension, and all that that entails; perhaps even to encountering alternatives of ourselves. The cosmos has turned out to be a far bigger and more interesting place than we thought. This insight is one which we share with many of our ancestors down through the ages.

Time travel

The theoretical evidence in favour of time travel is considerable. The only objections are variations on the causality paradox. This, I believe, has been sufficiently countered by the existence of the multiverse, in which all causality paradoxes vanish immediately. Yet a time traveller's future actions are not proscribed in any way. In particular, there is no compulsion to follow some predetermined course of action. In travelling through time, the futures of both the time traveller's universes (his original and his destination) are unknowable from the point at which he began to move backwards in the first and at which he arrives in the second, satisfying the condition of indeterminacy in both. It seems that Steven Spielberg's time traveller Dr Emmett Brown may well be right – your future really is whatever you make it.

There is, however, one question I have avoided until now. If time travel is possible, where are the time travellers? There are a number of possibilities. The most obvious and pessimistic of these is that life on Earth may simply not survive long enough for the technology to evolve. This particular future we are at liberty to choose or, it is to be hoped, avoid. Yet the absence of time travellers need not indicate anything nearly so sinister. It is possible that they have been here, and are here now, but have been discreet about their presence in order to ensure that they return to something closely approximating the future universe of their departure. A further possibility is simply that none has arrived in this particular universe. Any whom we despatch in the future will arrive in alternative universes. Perhaps the final answer lies in a combination of these.

Naturally, I for one would be most willing to welcome any such temporal voyager, provided that he or she was willing to provide proof in the form of advanced technology, or better still a few trips to the past and future. Yet to hope blindly for some super-descendant to provide us with a universal panacea to our present problems is as naively optimistic as expecting some sufficiently advanced, and benevolent, alien culture to stumble upon us. We must face the challenges by ourselves, and on our own terms. The challenge of space-time travel in particular is one we decline at the risk of our ultimate demise.

You are here

It seems, then, that it is not enough to know where and when you are, but you must also know which, amongst all the 'infinite' alternatives, you are. The universe is bigger than our ancestors could ever have dreamt, and may yet be bigger still. Fortunately, by now you should be so inured to having your horizons broadened, or maybe simply stunned by the vastnesses, that another experience of this kind is not so disturbing as to be rejected out of hand.

As for the fifth dimension, it provides a place through which space-time curves. It provides, also, a direction into which we can stack alternative universes – other cycles of our own universe, each as rich and complex as our own. Incidentally, it also provides us with a 'simple' resolution of the classic time travel 'paradox'. And, as we have seen, the fifth dimension itself is very probably curved! But in what? A sixth, yes, but what this may be, I will not conjecture – at least for the time being!

Appendix A: Four-Space

The Lorentz transformation (Minkowski's representation)
For simplicity it has been assumed throughout that z is the direction of motion.

$$x = x'$$
$$y = y'$$
$$z = (z' - v\,t')\,\gamma$$
$$ict = ic\left(t' - \frac{z'v}{c^2}\right)\gamma$$

where i is the square root of -1, and γ is the Lorentz factor given by

$$\gamma = \frac{1}{\left(1 - \frac{v^2}{c^2}\right)^{\frac{1}{2}}}$$

Lorentz invariant four vectors

Distance

$$\underline{R} = (x, y, z, ict)$$

which gives immediately the Lorentz transform invariant distance

$$s = (\Delta x^2 + \Delta y^2 + \Delta z^2 - (c.\Delta t)^2)^{\frac{1}{2}}$$
$$= (d^2 - c.\Delta t^2)^{\frac{1}{2}}$$

where Δx, Δy, and Δz denote distances in the x, y and z directions respectively and d is the normal three-space distance. Alternatively

$$\underline{R} = (\underline{r}, ict)$$

where $\underline{r}$ is the usual three-space position vector. Commonly, the first three components of a four-vector are the same as the three-space one of Newton – an example of how little difference there is between the two relativities.

Velocity

In Newtonian mechanics velocity is derived by differentiating the position with respect to time. The relative nature of time in Einstein's relativity appears at first glance to pose something of a problem. The solution is to use the 'proper time' τ, the time measured by an observer attached to the moving object. This has the advantage that $\Delta x = \Delta y = \Delta z = 0$, and also that the proper time τ is orthogonal to the other three axes; which is an intrinsic property of τ in Newtonian mechanics, considered as the fourth Euclidean ordinate.

Differentiating using the proper time gives the four-velocity

$$\underline{U} = \gamma(u)(u_x, u_y, u_z, 1) = \gamma(u)(\underline{u}, 1)$$

where $\underline{u}$ is the familiar three-space velocity of Newton.

Acceleration

Again, this is obtained by differentiating the four-velocity with respect to the proper time. This gives

$$\underline{A} = (\underline{a}, 0)$$

where $\underline{a}$ is the three-space acceleration of Newton. This result is immediately obvious from the above comments and the fact that the fourth component of the four-velocity was a constant.

Momentum

$$\underline{P} = \left(p_x, p_y, p_z, \frac{iE}{c}\right)$$

This gives immediately the Lorentz transformation invariant four-momentum

$$P = \left(p^2 - \frac{E^2}{c^2}\right)^{\frac{1}{2}}$$

where p is the magnitude of three-momentum of Newtonian mechanics. The conservation both of three-momentum and of mass-energy is contained within in the conservation of four-momentum.

Note: upper-case characters indicate quantities associated with four-dimensional quantities, and lower-case, three-dimensional. Vector quantities are distinguished from scalars by underlining.

Appendix B: Entropy

Entropy is defined as

$$S = -\Sigma \, p \, \log_2(p)$$

where p is the probability of an event and the sum is over all possible events.

Appendix C: Dirac's Derivation of Negative Mass-Energy

In classical Newtonian physics the energy E' of an object is given by:

$$E' = \tfrac{1}{2}mv^2$$

where m is its mass and v is its velocity. As both mass and any quantity squared must be positive, the energy also must be positive. Classical Newtonian momentum (three-vector p) is simply the product of the mass and velocity:

$$p = mv$$

Both classical energy and momentum are conserved. In relativistic Einsteinian physics, four-momentum, P, is of the form (px, py, pz, iE/c). It is now this four-momentum, momentum-energy, that is conserved. As a four-vector its magnitude is Lorentz invariant. If in one frame of reference, the rest frame, an object is at rest:

$$P^2 = m_0^2 c^2$$

where m is now the rest mass. In a frame in which it is moving:

$$P^2 = p^2 - \frac{E^2}{c^2}$$

where p is just the magnitude of Newton's three-momentum, and E is the corresponding energy. Each component of P is conserved, which consequently implies the conservation of both mass-energy and momentum, similarly to Newtonian mechanics. Additionally, as P is invariant, the last two equations must be equal, i.e. after rearranging

$$E^2 = m_0^2 c^4 + p^2 c^2$$

We are at liberty to take either the positive or negative square root of the right-hand side for the energy; the latter of these gives rise to negative mass energies.

Appendix D: Complex Relativistic Rotation

In flat, Euclidean space rotations are represented by the transformation:

$$\begin{pmatrix} x \\ y \end{pmatrix} = \begin{pmatrix} \cos\theta & \sin\theta \\ -\sin\theta & \cos\theta \end{pmatrix} \begin{pmatrix} x' \\ y \end{pmatrix}$$

where θ is the angle of rotation.

The Lorentz transformation is a complex rotation represented by:

$$\begin{pmatrix} z \\ ict \end{pmatrix} - \begin{pmatrix} \cos i\theta & \sin i\theta \\ -\sin i\theta & \cos i\theta \end{pmatrix} \begin{pmatrix} z' \\ ict' \end{pmatrix}$$

where

$$i = \tan^{-1}\left(\frac{iv}{c}\right)$$

This is not exactly the same as a real rotation as it obeys the identity

$$z^2 - (ct)^2 = 1$$

which results in the more common alternative expression for the Lorentz transformation involving hyperbolic trigonometric functions of real angles:

$$\begin{pmatrix} z' \\ ct' \end{pmatrix} = \begin{pmatrix} \cosh\theta & -\sinh\theta \\ -\sinh\theta & \cosh\theta \end{pmatrix} \begin{pmatrix} z \\ ct \end{pmatrix}$$

The above complex form is simply the Minkowskian equivalent of this.

Bibliography

Antimatter

HANNES, Alfén, *World–Antiworlds: Antimatter in Cosmology*, San Francisco: W. H. Freeman and Co., 1966.

Cosmology

BERRY, M., *Principles of Cosmology and Gravitation*, Cambridge, Cambridge University Press, 1976.

HENBEST, Nigel, *The Mysterious Universe*, London, Ebury Press, 1981.

SCIAMA, D. W., *Modern Cosmology*, Cambridge, Cambridge University Press, 1971.

HINCKFUSS, Ian, *The Existence of Space and Time*, Oxford, Clarendon Press, 1975.

NARLIKAR, Jayant, *The Structure of the Universe*, Oxford, Oxford University Press, 1977.

TAYLOR, Edwin F. and John A. Wheeler, *Spacetime Physics*, San Francisco, W. H. Freeman & CO., 1966.

TOBEN, Bob, *Space-Time and Beyond*, New York, Dutton, 1974.

WALD, R. M., *Space, Time and Gravity*, Chicago, University of Chicago Press, 1977.

WEINBERG, Steven, *The First Three Minutes*, New York, Basic Books, 1977; London, Deutsch, 1977.

Entropy

COVENEY, Peter and Roger Highfield, *The Arrow of Time*, W. H. Allen, 1990.

HALL, G. G. and S. B. Jones, 'Information and Entropy for a Planar Box', *American Journal of Physics*, Vol. 41, pp. 213–216, February 1973.

Geometry

ABBOTT, Edwin A., *Flatland: A Romance of Many Dimensions*, originally published 1884, various reprints available.

BURGER, Dionys (trans. Cornelie J. Rheinboldt), *Sphereland*, New York, T. Y. Crowell, 1965.

Gravity

MISNER, C. W., K. S. Thorne and J. A. Wheeler, *Gravitation*, San Francisco, W. H. Freeman, 1974.

NICOLSON, Iain, *Gravity, Black Holes and the Universe*, Newton Abbot, David and Charles, 1981.

WEINBERG, Steven, *Gravitation and Cosmology: Principles and Applications of the General Theory of Relativity*, Wiley, New York and Chichester, 1972.

Paradoxes

GARDNER, Martin, *Gotcha: Paradoxes to Puzzle and Delight*, San Francisco, W. H. Freeman & Co., 1982.

KORZYBSKI, Alfred, *Science and Sanity*, Science Press, 1933.

MARTIN, Robert L. (ed.), *The Paradox of the Liar*, New Haven, Yale University Press, 1970.

MOTZ, Lloyd and Anneta Duveen, *Essentials of Astronomy*, Columbia University Press, 1966.

Quantum mechanics

GRIBBIN, John, *In Search of Schrödinger's Cat*, New York, Bantam, 1986; London, Black Swan, 1986.

MATTHEWS, P. T., *Introduction to Quantum Mechanics*, Maidenhead, McGraw-Hill, 1985.

Relativity

ALONSO, Marcelo and Edward J. Finn, *Fundamental University Physics*, London, Addison-Wesley, 1966.

EINSTEIN, Albert, *Relativity: The Special and General Theory*, London, Methuen, 1960.

MOOK, Delo E. and Thomas Vargish, *Inside Relativity*, Princeton, Princeton University Press, 1974.

KAUFMANN, W. J., *The Cosmic Frontiers of General Relativity*, London, Penguin, 1979.

RINDLER, Wolfgang, *Essential Relativity: Special, General, and Cosmological*, Dallas, Texas, Southwest Center for Advanced Studies, 1969.

SCHWINGER, Julian, *Einstein's Legacy*, New York: W. H. Freeman/Scientific American, 1986.

WILL, Clifford, *Was Einstein Right?*, New York, Basic Books, 1986.

Time

DAVIES, P. C. W., *The Physics of Time Asymmetry*, Berkeley, University of California Press, 1974.

GARDNER, Martin, 'On the Contradiction of Time Travel', Mathematical Games Department, *Scientific American*, May 1974.

GOLDWIRTH, D.S., M.J. Perry and T. Piran, *General Relativity and Gravitation*, Vol. 25, No. 1, 1993.

GRIBBIN, John, *In Search of the Edge of Time*, London, Bantam Press, 1992.

HAWKING, Stephen, *A Brief History of Time*, London, Bantam Press, 1988.

REDMOUNT, I., 'Wormholes, Time Travel and Quantum Gravity', *New Scientist*, 28 April 1990.

WHITROW, G. J., *The Nature of Time*, New York, Holt, Rinehart and Winston, 1973; London, Pelican/Penguin, 1973.

Index

absolutes 31
  time 60
  velocity 35ff
absolutely stationary frame
  36
acceleration 44, 49, 63, 69,
  75, 88
  constant 51ff
  external 42, 51
  four 149
  internal 51
accuracy 34
action 111ff
  Lorentz invariant 111,
  112
addition of
  of speed (velocity) 33ff,
  40, 42ff
advance of the perihelion
  77
age of the universe 12, 21,
  112
air resistance 13, 49
alternative realities 140
alternative universes 97ff,
  102, 105, 140, 146
analogies 3, 53, 142
Andromeda 49
anti-electron 124
anti-particles 125
Aristotle 8
arrow of time 103, 106ff,
  141
artificial gravity 51
atomic nuclei 81
atoms 81, 116ff
attraction 70
average density of matter
  78
average energy 127
axioms 24ff

Baade and Zwicky 84
background temperature
  20

backwards in time 67, 96,
  102
balance of forces 70, 75, 82
balloon model 101ff
beginning of universe 101ff
beginning of time 12, 101ff
bending of light 64, 76
bent universe 30, 69, 77ff
Big Bang 12, 20, 101ff,
  103
billiard-ball model 96, 105
black hole 79ff, 85ff, 141
  Crab Nebula 84
  in a curved space-time
  104
  density (surface density)
  86
  distortion of space 87ff
  entropy of 113
  escape velocity 85
  event horizon 85ff, 90,
  92
  galaxy-sized 89
  size 88
  tidal forces of 88
  trip 91ff
  universe 93ff, 102
blue event horizon 90
boundary 56

'c' see speed of light
caesium clocks 75
causality paradox see paradox, father and son
centre of mass 13
centre of the universe 102
charged particles 70
chemical properties 123
Cherenkov, P., radiation 64
circles 57
circumference 56, 73
classical theories 96
clocks
  caesium 75
  synchronized 76

closed loop in time 104
closed surface 74
collapse of the universe 82,
  87, 103, 141
collapse star 95
colour 17
communication 93, 126
complex rotation 152
conservation
  of energy 151
  of mass-energy 51, 63,
  151
  of momentum 63, 151
constant of gravitation 80
continuous space and
  continuous time 148
cooling
  of planets and stars 15
  by radiation 82
  of stellar clouds 15
  of the universe 12
cosmic censor 137
cosmology 78, 101ff
Crab Nebula 84
cumulative effect 135
cumulative gravity 70, 83
curvature 25, 73ff
  black hole 104
  determining 57
  four-dimensional 74
  gravitational 73
  infinite 87
  negative 57
  positive 57, 102
  space-time 134
  of the universe 30, 69,
  77ff
  zero 57
curved space 56ff, 69
cycle in time 102ff

dark galaxies 87
dark stars 87
density 81, 83, 86ff
  average of stars 27ff

of matter in space 26
of the universe *see*
     universe, fate of
deterministic 138
different space-time contin-
     uum 96, *see also*
     alternative universe
Dirac, P. A. M. 121, 124,
     151
direction 25, 113
   of motion 38, 92
   radial 92ff
discrete 96, 109ff
   energy levels 122ff
   orbits 122
disorder 108, 109
distance 19, 33ff, 55, 53ff
   four-space 47ff, 148
   local measure of 32
   shrinkage of 46, 50
   three-space 46
   units of 49
drag 70
draughtboard model 108ff
dust cloud 19

Earth 79
   escape velocity 79, 81
eccentricity 77
edge 56
Einstein, Albert 32
   general relativity 69ff,
     75ff
   special theory of relativity
     8, 11, 37ff, 39, 52,
     63, 69
electric charge 136
electromagnetic
   radiation 16ff
   repulsion 81
   waves 69
   waves, four-space-time
     geodesics 134
electron 12, 70, 81, 109,
     122
energies discrete 122ff
energy 43, 82, 106, 122ff
   average 127
   average inter-molecular
     127
   conservation of 51, 63,
     151
   level 122ff
   of motion 121
   negative 121, 123ff
   Newtonian 151
   positive 121

relativistic 151
   and temperature 127ff
   total 121
   total in universe 112
entropy 106ff, 122, 150
   actual 112ff
   of a black hole 116
   in a contracting universe
     113ff
   example of 106ff
   limits of 109
   maximum 108, 112ff
   model simple 108ff
Epimenides 23ff
equivalence
   of acceleration and
     gravity 32
   gravitation and inertia
     88, 91, 92
   principle of 70ff
   of space and time 60
error (in Newtonian
     mechanics) 33, 39
escape velocity 79ff
   of a black hole 85
   at Earth's surface 79, 81
   of Jupiter 81
   of moon 82
   of a neutron star 85
   of the sun 81
   of a white dwarf 85
eternity 104
Euclidean four-space-time
     143
Euclidean space 25, 56, 73,
     104, 131
Euclidean universe 25ff
event horizon 85ff, 90, 92
   see also black holes
everyday experience 32
evidence
   for general relativity 75ff
   for special relativity 52
   for time travel 37
evolution
   of galaxies 13ff
   of stars 15ff
   of the universe 12ff, 29
exclusion principle 110,
     124
expanding box 117
expansion of the universe
     12ff, 29, 101, 141
experimental verification
     24

faster than light *see* FTL

father and son paradox
     22ff, 105, 137ff, 147ff
fifth dimension 137ff
finite 56
five-dimensional model
     142
five-dimensional hyper-
     sphere 143
fixed stars 35
flat region of space 75
flat space *see* Euclidean
     space
flatlanders 54, 73, 131ff
force 61, 69ff, 134
   of attraction 70
   balance of 70, 75, 82
   electromagnetic 69ff
   gravity 69ff
   nuclear 69ff
   strong nuclear 69ff
   tidal 88, 91ff
   weak nuclear 69ff
forces of nature, four 69ff
four-acceleration 60
four-dimensional 46, 53ff,
     129
   balloon 101ff, 141
   curvature 74
   hypersphere 101ff
four-radius maximum 143
four-space 47ff, 74, 148
four-space-time 133
four-vectors 148
four-velocity 60
fourth dimension 46ff, 53ff
free fall 51, 75ff
free space 71
frequency 84
friction 13, 49
frontiers of science 10
frozen in time 39, 91
FTL 62ff, 128
   particles 65
fundamental particle 110
fusion 13, 15, 16

galaxies 140
   evolution 13ff
   dark 87
   light from distant 17ff
   nearest neighbouring 49
   origins 12
   proto- 12
   recession of 19ff
galaxy-sized black hole 89
gas 127
gas clouds 12

gauge theory 126, 135
general relativity 69ff, 75ff
geodesic 134
geometry 112, 129, 135,
  145
  space-time 78
  universe's 20
gravitation, Newton's
  theory of 85
gravitational
  condensation 15
  length contraction 73
  Lorentz factor 73
  time dilation 72
  well 74, 90
gravity 41, 69ff, 72, 75,
  79ff, 88, 134
  artificial 51
  constant of 80
  cumulative 70, 83
  curvature 73
  inertia equivalence 70ff,
    88, 91, 92
  infinite 125
  inverse square law 28
  red shift 90
  versus electromagnetism
    82
great arcs 36, 132, 134

Hawking, Stephen 111,
  137, 143
heat 82
heat death of the sun 107
heat death of the universe
  107
Heisenberg, W. 111
  uncertainty principle 111
higher dimensions 25
history, personal 137, 138
hole electron 124
horizons, event see event
  horizon
horizons, human 140
Hubble's constant 19ff
hydrogen atom 70
hypersphere 74, 94, 98,
  101ff
hyperspherical balloon 31,
  98
hyperspherical surface 93

imaginary
  angles 131
  journey 45, 49, 62
  journey to a black hole
    91ff

number 58, 64
time 65ff
indeterminacy 105
inertial observer 33ff
infinite
  brightness of night sky
    24
  density 51
  series 24
  speed 30, 49
  universe 22
infinite thinness 39
infinitely thin universe 63
infinity 22ff
inflation 103
initial speed 88
inside planets 80, 81
invariance of four momen-
  tum 121
invariants 36, 47, 148, 149
inverse square law
  for gravity 28
  for light 26

journeys, imaginary
  to Andromeda 49
  to Proxima Centauri 45

kinetic energy 121

Landau, L. 83
Laplace, P. S. 85
length contraction 38ff,
  131
  gravitational 73
length of a moving object
  38
length of a stationary object
  38
life 107
lift 71
light 16ff
  barrier 67
  bending of by gravity 65,
    76
  speed in vacuum 16
  visible 17
  waves 109
local measure of distance
  32
local passage of time 32
logic 23
Lorentz, H. A.
  contraction 66
  factor 37ff
  factor gravitational 73

invariant 60, 111, 112,
  148
time dilation 60
transform 37ff, 64, 148,
  152
transform as a rotation
  131

magnetic field 84
mass 13, 15, 41ff, 63, 81
  centre of 13
  rest 41ff
mass-energy 16, 77, 121,
  151
  conservation of 51, 63
  equivalence 12
  negative 67, 151
  origin 103
maximum entropy 108,
  112ff
measurement 33
Mercury 77
Michelson, A. 11
Michelson-Morley
  experiment 35ff
Milky Way 21
Minkowski, H. 48
  spacetime 48ff, 50, 149,
  152
model 55
  balloon 101ff
  billiard-ball 96, 105
  draughtboard 108ff
  five-dimensional 142
  five-dimensional hyper-
    sphere 143ff
  four-dimensional hyper-
    spherical balloon 98,
    144
  gas in perfectly elastic
    sided box 110,
    116ff
  'onion' 143
  rubber sheet 74, 75, 87,
    88
  of the universe 25, 31,
    117
momentum 43
momentum, four- 149
moon, escape velocity of
  81
Morley, E. W. 35ff
motion 129ff
  relative 33ff
moving observer 33ff
multiverse 137, 138

negative
    distances 47ff
    energy 121, 123ff
    mass-energy 67, 151
    time 65ff
neutron star 95, 83ff
    Crab Nebula 84
neutronium 86
neutrons 12, 81
Newton, Sir Isaac
    theories 76ff, 85
Newtonian
    energy 151
    mechanics 42
    physics 111
    relativity 33ff
    time 60
night sky 24ff
novas 15, 82
now 20-1
nuclear energy 11
nuclear forces 69ff
nuclear fusion 82
nucleus 122
numbers, imaginary 58, 64
numbers, real 58

observer 33ff
    accelerated 69
    in constant relative
        velocity see inertial
    inertial 33ff, 69, 132
    moving see inertial
    stationary 33ff
Olbers, H. W. M., paradox
    of 24ff
one-dimensional 53
open universe 103
orbit 35, 75ff, 90
    discrete 122
orbiting spacecraft 76
origin of the universe 12,
    21, 102

paradox 22ff, 68, 141
    father and son (causality)
        22ff, 105, 137ff, 147
    lying Cretans 23
    Olbers' 24ff
    twin 44ff, 133
particles 12, 96
    charged 70
payload 51
perihelion, advance of 77
personal histories 137, 138
photons 69, 76
physical science 24

Planck, M., constant 111
planets 13, 81
    of other stars 16
Pluto 20, 77
Poincaré, J. H., dilemma of
    116
position 111
positive curvature 102
    of universe 74, 78
positive energy 121
positron 124
possibilities, number of
    109ff
possibility 107ff
principle of equivalence
    70ff
probability 107ff, 118, 138
proper time 50, 59ff, 66,
    78, 91
proton 12, 70, 81
Proxima Centauri 45, 62
    nearest star 20
    travel time to 46
pseudo sub-light velocity
    65ff
pulsars 83, see also neutron
    stars

quantum discreteness 96ff,
    111ff
quantum theory 105

radial direction 92ff
radio pulses 83
radio signals 83
radius 81, 101, 142
real numbers 58
recession 30
red shift 16ff, 29, 30, 31
    gravitational 90
relative motion 130
relative time 32
relativistic thermodynamics
    128
relativistic travel 43ff
rest mass 41ff, 51, 63, 121,
    128
reverse time 67, 96, 126ff,
    139
reverse time travel 9
rotation 84, 95, 130, 132,
    133, 152
    for artificial gravity 51
    complex 152
    of galaxies 13ff
    of spacecraft 51
    of stars 13ff

of the universe 12ff
rubber sheet model 74, 75,
    87, 88

scale 26, 60ff, 70
    human 112
Schmidt, M., red shift 18
Schwartzchild, M. 85, 92
    radius 85ff, 103, 141
    wormholes 100, 137
semantics, general 24
shortest distance 134
signature 48
singularity 94ff, 97, 102,
    141
    circular 95ff
    four-space-time 99
    in space-time 94ff
    in three-space 99
Sirius 83
Sirius B 83
sixth dimension 147
size of the universe 143
special theory of relativity
        see Einstein, special
        theory of relativity
space 12, 32, 101, 102
    curved 69
    distortion of 87ff
    flat region of 75
    free 71
    and time 61
    travel 145
space-like properties 92
space-time 47ff, 61, 74,
    133, 148
    curvature 134
spacecraft 63, 129
    orbiting 76
spectra 18, 90
speed of light ('L') 88, 91,
    103, 112
    constancy of 17, 34
    in vacuum 16
    variable 37
sphere 74
    surface of 56, 132
spherical wave front 26
spin, sub-atomic 67
stars 13ff
    average density of 27ff
    dark 87
    distribution of 25
    evolution of 15ff
    fixed 35
    life cycle 15ff
    nearest 20

power source 15ff
static universe 26ff
stationary observer 33ff
stellar clouds 12
straight line 56
strong nuclear force 69ff
sub-light velocity 43, 59,
    62, 66ff
sun 16, 87
super-light velocity 66, 92
super string theory 139,
    140
supernovas 15, 82
surface 55
    area 73
    closed 74
    of a sphere 132
symmetry 67, 80, 93
    spherical 95
synchronized clocks 76

telescopes 16
temperature 15, 127ff
    background 20
ten dimensions 139
thermodynamics, relativistic
    128
three-dimensional 54
three-space 46, 47
    distance 46
    flat 144
three-vectors 148
tidal effect 71
tidal forces 88, 91ff
tides 71
time 12, 32, 33ff, 53ff, 101
    absolute 60
    arrow of 103, 106ff, 141
    backwards in 67, 96, 102
    beginning of 12, 101ff
    closed loop in 104
    dilation 38, 39ff, 52, 91,
        131ff
        gravitational 72
        verification of 75
    in units of distance 49
    -like properties 92
    /light barrier 93
    local passage of 32
    Newtonian see absolute
    relative 32
    reverse 126ff
    travel 7, 31ff, 62, 145
        impossibility of 22

major objection to 23
travellers 22, 146
total eclipse 76
travel 62
    to a black hole 91ff
    Einsteinian 49ff
    Newtonian 49ff
    relativistic 43ff
    time see time, travel
triangle 57, 131ff
trip to a black hole 91ff
tunnel in space-time 100
twin paradox 44ff, 133
two-dimensional universe
    54, 129

unbounded and finite space
    102
uncertainty 96
unified theory 136
uniform infinite universe
    24ff
uniform relative motion 33
universal constants see
    invariants
universe
    age of 12, 21, 112
    alternative 96ff, 102,
        105, 140, 146
    average density of 78, 87
    beginning of 12, 101ff
    black hole 93ff
    centre of 102
    collapsing 103
    curvature of 30, 69, 77ff
    cycle 102ff
    deterministic 138
    energy in 112
    entropy in a contracting
        113ff
    evolution 12ff
    expansion of 12ff, 29
    fate of 70, 87
    finite bounded 31
    finite size of 28
    flat, Euclidean 30
    geometry 20
    history 12ff
    infinite 24
    maximum size of 145
    models of 25, 54, 117
    open 103
    origin of 12, 21, 102
    positive curvature 74, 78

second 97ff
size of 143
static 26ff
third 100
two-dimensional model
    54, 129
typical part of 25
ultimate collapse of 103
volume of 140

vectors 54
    addition of 54
    four- 148
    subtraction of 54
    three- 148
velocity 33ff, 80, 111
    absolute 35ff
    addition of 33ff, 40, 42ff
    changes of see
        acceleration
    four- 149
    of escape see escape
        velocity
    of light see speed of light
    limiting 42, 46
    small 69
    sub-light 48, 59, 62
    super-light 66, 92
    see also speed of light
Venus 20
Voyagers 45

water 64, 127
wave-like properties 96
wave-particle duality 122
waves 96
    electromagnetic 16ff
    frequency of 16ff
    length 17
    light 109
    oceanic 17
    in water 64
weight 41ff
Wells, H. G. 7
white dwarf 83
white hole 79ff, 97ff, 102,
    141
work 106
wormholes 100, 137

you are here 10ff, 21, 146

zero length 39